William Harwar Parker

Questions on Practical Seamanship

Together With Harbor Routine and Evolutions

William Harwar Parker

Questions on Practical Seamanship
Together With Harbor Routine and Evolutions

ISBN/EAN: 9783744797962

Printed in Europe, USA, Canada, Australia, Japan

Cover: Foto ©Andreas Hilbeck / pixelio.de

More available books at **www.hansebooks.com**

QUESTIONS ON PRACTICAL SEAMANSHIP;

TOGETHER WITH

HARBOR ROUTINE AND EVOLUTIONS;

PREPARED FOR THE MIDSHIPMEN OF THE C. S. NAVY,

BY

WM. H. PARKER,

COMMANDING C. S. SCHOOL-SHIP PATRICK HENRY.

RICHMOND:
MACFARLANE AND FERGUSSON, PRINTERS.
1863.

PREFACE.

This little book is published for the use of the Midshipmen of the C. S. Navy. It has been prepared from notes collected by me while attached to the U. S. Naval Academy, Annapolis, as Instructor in Naval Tactics and Seamanship.

Having left the greater part of my MSS. in the hands of the enemy, I am compelled to publish this work in an incomplete form—at some future day I hope to issue it in a more creditable manner.

The Part on Harbor Routine, and the plan of Part III, is somewhat new, and suggested itself to me while employed in teaching at the U. S. Naval Academy. Questions are asked and the Answers omitted in order to cause the Student *to think;* and to give the Instructor an opportunity of explaining *the philosophy* of Seamanship and Naval Discipline.

 C. S. PATRICK HENRY,
  JAMES RIVER,
   September 28*th*, 1863.

Part I.

RIGGING. QUESTIONS ON.

Knot a Rope-Yarn.
Make a Fox—a Spanish Fox—a Knittle—a Figure of Eight Knot—Two Half-Hitches—a Square Knot—a Bowline Knot—a Bowline on the Bight—a Running Bowline—a Timber Hitch—a Fisherman's Bend—a Rolling Bend—a Carrick Bend—a Cat's-Paw—a Sheet Bend—a Back-Wall Hitch—a Rolling Hitch—a Selvagee Strap—a Pudding for a mast or yard—a Turk's Head—a Clove Hitch.
What are the uses of the above foxes, bends, knots, hitches, &c.?
Make a Short Splice—a Long Splice—a Cut Splice—an Eye Splice—a Flemish Eye—an Artificial Eye.
Explain the uses of the above.
Worm and Serve a Rope; Parcel a Rope.
What is the object of worming, Parcelling and serving?
Put on a Throat and Quarter Seizing.
Sheepshank a Rope. When is it done?
What is woolding?
Put a Strand in a Rope.
To Wall and Crown.
Make a Matthew Walker Knot—a Spritsail Sheet Knot—a Shroud Knot—a French Shroud Knot—a Single Diamond Knot—a Double Diamond Knot—a Stopper Knot.
What are the above knots used for?
Making Sennet, Gaskets and Mats—Point and Graft a Rope. Why is it done?
Pass a Rose Lashing.
Make a Grommet. What is its use?
What is a Cleat?
Name the different parts of a block.
What is a Double block? a Fiddle block? a Shoe block? a Sister block? a shoulder block? a Dead-Eye? a Heart? a Thimble? an Euphroe? a Tail block? a Snatch block? a Purchase block? a Top block? a Cat block?
Explain the uses of the above.
What is a Nun Buoy, and what is its use?
Bend a Buoy Rope.
Pudding the ring of an anchor. Why is it done?

Reeve a Single Whip—a Gun Tackle Purchase—a Luff Tackle—a Top Burton—a Whip and Runner—a Runner and Tackle—a Threefold Purchase.

Name some of the uses of the above.

What is Hawser-laid rope? Shroud-laid rope? Water-laid rope? Cable-laid rope?

What is Spun Yarn? Marline? Hambro' line? What used for?

Heave the log and lead, and steer.

Get on board and rig Sheers. Show how the Sheer-Head lashing is passed.

What are the *Shoes* for? What are parbuckles?

Take in the Masts and Bowsprit. Show how the *garland* is made and lashed on.

Rig the Foremast. Turn in a dead eye. What is the use of the trussel-trees? Why take out the *after* chock in preference to the forward one? What are the lower cross-trees and their use? What are the bolsters? Why are the fore and aft stays fitted with lashing eyes? and why put over last?

Stay the foremast and set up the rigging.

Rig the Bowsprit. Show how the Gammoning is passed.

Get the Tops over.

Get on board, rig and fid a topmast.

How do you rattle down the rigging?

What is the distance between the ratlines?

Get on board and rig the Jib-boom.

What is a *traveller*, and its use?

What is a Dolphine-Striker, and its use?

Get on board and rig the Flying Jib-boom.

Send up, rig and fid the Top-Gallant masts.

State particularly how the mast-rope is rove, (either double or single.)

Why is the fore and aft stay put over first?

Rig the Spritsail Yard.

What is the use of a Spritsail Yard?

What is meant by "canting the Spritsail Yard?"

Why is it done after tacking?

Are Spritsail Yards much used?

Get on board, rig, and send up the Lower Yards.

Get on board, rig, and cross a Topsail Yard.

Rig a Top-Gallant Yard and cross it.

Rig a Spanker Boom and Gaff.

Reeve all running rigging and studding sail gear.

Where are the chain cables stowed—how marked, and bent?

Name the different parts of an anchor.

Explain the manner of heaving up an anchor—passing the Messenger—putting on nippers—bitting and unbitting—catting and fishing, &c.

Fit Cat-Stopper and Shank Painter.

Secure an anchor for sea.

How let go an anchor?

What is a Deck Stopper? a Dog Stopper? a Bitt Stopper? a Trip Stopper? a Wing Stopper, and a Ring Stopper? and what their various uses?

What is a Compressor, and what its use?

How would you ship and unship a rudder?

How are the Wheel Ropes rove?

Explain the Steering gear of this ship; or the ship last served in.

Make out a Quarter and Watch Bill for an Iron Clad mounting two 7 inch Brook Guns and two 9 inch Dahlgren Shell Guns; or for the ship last served in.

Make out a Fire Bill for the above.

How fit clothes lines and hammock girtlines?

How do you clear hawse?

How is the foremast of this ship rigged? the topmast? the top-gallant mast? the gaff?

How was the mast gotten in?

How is the fore yard rigged? the topsail yard? the top-gallant yard?

How is the fore yard sent up and down? the topsail yard? the top-gallant yard?

How is the top-gallant mast sent up and down? the topmast? the gaff?

How is the running rigging rove?

How are the sails loosed and furled?

How are they bent and unbent?

How are they reefed?

How are the anchors hove up and secured?

Where are the chains stowed?

How are our Wheel Ropes rove?

How and where are the Relieving Tackles hooked?

Part II.

HARBOR ROUTINE.

Note.—In the 2d and 3d Parts the "Orders," (supposed to be given by the Officer of the Deck,) are printed in italics.

DAILY ROUTINE IN PORT.

The ordinary routine in port is as follows:

The officer of the morning watch having read the "morning orders," directs the Quartermaster to have the music up, and gun ready, before daylight. At that time, he directs them to "go on with the music," and the gun is fired. He directs the Midshipman of the watch to call the Forward Officers and Master's Mates, and to tell the Boatswain to "call all hands and pipe the hammocks up, (and if clothes are to be scrubbed, to "call all hands and scrub and wash clothes.") The Boatswain will do so at the last tap of the drum, and in ten minutes thereafter, the hammocks should be reported up by the Mates of the lower decks.

The Mates receive their orders as to what is to be done with their decks—the market boat is called away and sent with the stewards; the hammock-cloths hauled over and the decks swept down; if the awnings are spread, they will be triced up; and all rigging will be laid up clear of the decks.

The crew now scrub their clothes; the starboard watch on the spar deck, and the port watch on the main deck; and when a reasonable time has elapsed, the clothes-lines are overhauled down, the clothes stopped on, and the lines triced up again. The decks are then scrubbed, as ordered, and washed down at the command of the officer of the Deck.

The men should not be allowed to draw water over the bows, from the gangways, or from the chains; nor should they be allowed *outside* of the ship at all.

The top-keepers should be sent aloft to put the tops in order after the clothes are triced up. They should be ordered aloft *together*, and when they have finished their work, should notify the Officer of the Deck, so that he may order them *down* together.

The decks should be dried down by 7:30 A. M. and the ship washed off outside. The carpenters wash from the "bends" down, *after the decks are dried.*

The yards should now be squared, (observing that the men going aloft are dressed alike,) and if the decks are dry enough, the awnings spread and rigging flemished down. Roll up the hammock-cloths, clean bright work, haul the boom cover over neatly &c., &c.

The "tea-water" is reported by the ship's cook at 7 bells, and is served out by order of the Officer of the Deck.

If sails are to be loosed, yards crossed, or masts sent up at 8 o'clock, preparations must be made beforehand, and the yards are not squared until after the evolution. A few minutes before 8, the boat's crews are sent aft to prepare their boats for lowering, and the music is called. When the "call" is beaten, the pennant is shifted, and at 8 bells the boats are lowered, sails loosed, or yards crossed, colors hoisted, &c., &c., &c.

The Captain is always informed when the flag-ship makes signal to the squadron, and the *time* is reported to him, at 8 A. M., Meridian, and 8 P. M.

The command is now given to "pipe to breakfast," and the bum-boat is allowed to come alongside. The word is passed at the same time how the men are to dress.

The log is written up and signed, and the deck "turned over" to the Officer of the forenoon watch.

At 9, the hands are "turned to," decks swept down, and the drummer beats to quarters. After inspection, the divisions are exercised, marines drilled, &c.

A guard is always kept on deck until sunset, or evening quarters.

At 10, the regular boats are called away—the officers are notified, and in four or five minutes the boats shove off—the wardroom officers leaving the ship from the starboard side, the steerage officers from the port side.

After the divisions have been exercised, the men are set at work, as required.

At 11:30, the dinner is brought to the mast for inspection, decks swept down, and sails furled, or clothes piped down (if dry.) At Meridian, the boatswain pipes to dinner.

At 1, the hands are "turned to" and decks swept. The regular boats are sent, and work carried on as ordered. At 3, the regular boats are sent; at 3:30, tea-water reported and decks cleared up; and at 4, the boatswain pipes to supper, and passes the word to the men to "shift in blue;" the log is written, &c., &c., &c.

At 4:30, the hands are "turned to," and decks swept. Half an hour before sunset, the awnings are furled, rigging laid up, and, if clothes or hammocks are to be scrubbed, the lines are prepared for going up. At sunset the colors are hauled down, boats hoisted up, yards and masts sent down, (if required,) lines triced up, &c., &c.

The sunset boat leaves the ship before sunset, and shoves off from the shore when the colors are hauled down. The music is called five minutes before sunset, the "call" is beaten two or three minutes before. All sunset evolutions are performed at the third roll of the drum.

The men are mustered at quarters either before or after sunset. After the sunset-boat has been run up, the hammocks are piped down, and quarter deck awning housed, (if desired,) lightning conductors rigged out, &c., &c.

At dark, the necessary lights are lit and hoisted, and at 8 P. M., the music "beats off," the gun is fired, anchor watch set, and fires and lights reported out to the captain. At 9, the steerage lights are extinguished, and at 10, those of the wardroom.

The sentries are relieved every two hours by the sergeant of the Guard. After gun-fire they pass the call,. "All's well," every half hour. All boats are hailed after dark, and reported to the Officer of the Deck.

It is not customary to set an anchor-watch unless lying at single anchor. In that case, one of the main-topmen tends the drift land. The anchor watch is taken from the forecastle-men, if at single anchor; but the *sheet-anchors* are let go by the quarter gunners.

The gunners, besides having all ordnance stores, guns, &c., in his charge, has also the main yard, main rigging and sheet-anchors.

At night, the lights below should be inspected every half hour, by a Midshipman. The lights in the engine-room should be reported by the engineer of the watch at the same time.

QUESTION. At what hour is the reveille beat?
Q. At what hour is the tattoo beat?
Q. How would you calculate the time of day-light?
Q. How and why are the awnings triced up?
Q. What are the hammock-cloths, and how fitted?
Q. What is the "boom-cover?"
Q. What are the "morning orders?
Q. What are the top-keepers, and what is their particular duty?
Q. What is a "catamoran," and what is its use?
Q. How and why is rigging flemished down?
Q. What is the "tea-water," and why is it reported?
Q. Why is the dinner inspected by the Officer of the Deck?

Q. Where should the Officer of the Deck receive all reports from the crew?

Q. How are the watches usually divided in port?

Q. In a steam-frigate, who are on watch at night besides the Officer of the Deck?

Q. In what are the divisions exercised?

Q. What is meant by the "regular boats?"

Q. What light is carried in port?

ANSWER. By order of the Navy Department, a ship must carry a light, in a globular lantern, 20 feet above the deck, and placed in such a manner as to be visible all round the horizon.

QUESTION. How are the lightning conductors fitted?

Q. What lights are sometimes hoisted at the peak?

Q. What *answer* does a Flag Officer, Captain, Ward-Room Officer, Steerage Officer, or sailor, give when hailed in coming alongside at night?

Q. Why is it customary to beat the "call," before "rolling off," at 8 A. M., &c.?

Q. How is a Flag Officer's boat, or Captain's boat, distinguished in the day-time? (provided, the Flag Officer or Captain is *in the boat*.)

Q. At what time are colors hoisted?

Q. What is a "dog-vane?"

Q. What is meant by a "foul hawse?"

Q. What is an "elbow," a "round turn," &c.?

UPON "TAKING THE DECK" IN PORT.

Upon taking the deck in port, the Officer should ascertain whether any boats are away, and what boats are at the booms; if the men are at meals; the state of the hawse; if she has been kept clear of her anchor, (when lying at single anchor;) if the watch is set; man at the drift-lead; lights reported out; if the Captain is out of the ship, &c., &c., and whether there are any particular orders to be passed.

He should then assure himself that the yards are square, rigging stopped in, and all ship-shape *aloft*, that no ropes are towing overboard, no port laniards adrift; that boat-keepers are in the boats, colors and pendant clear and hoisted taut up, awnings properly set, and boom-cover hauled over, hammocks well stowed, bright work cleaned, decks swept down, boat's falls neatly stopped up, rigging flemished down, &c., &c., &c.

If at meals, that the meal pendant is up.

He should cause a good look-out kept for signals, and boats

approaching the ship, as well as arrivals and departures of vessels from the port.

He is accountable for the proper execution of all evolutions, and will be constantly on the alert.

It should be his constant care that the ship presents a creditable appearance "alow and aloft," and all his energies should be directed to effect it.

STOWING HAMMOCKS.

In stowing the hammocks, the men appointed for the purpose should refuse to take any hammock not properly lashed up. In former times it was customary to pass each hammock through a hoop before stowing it. They should be stowed so as to fill the nettings, and of an uniform height, numbers up and in. The starboard watch stow their hammocks on the starboard, the port watch on the port side, fore-castlemen and firemen forward, fore and main-topmen amidships, after-guard, mizen-topmen and marines aft. The steerage hammocks are stowed in the poop nettings, in a 74, and in the after part of the quarter-deck nettings in other vessels.

The hammock-cloths are hauled over as soon as the hammocks are stowed. After the decks are dried down, if the Officer wishes to "roll up" the hammock-cloths, he commands: *Stand by to bring in and roll up the hammock-cloths.* The order is repeated, and when the men are ready, *man the side*—the jack-stays are unrove and the cloths brought in together at the command *lay in;* they are then rolled up and laid on top of the hammocks together at the command *lay out;* when done, the command is given, *lay in,* and the men all come in together.

At the approach of rain, the command is given: *haul over the hammock-cloths,* and they are cut adrift and hauled smoothly over.

PIPING DOWN HAMMOCKS.

All hands having been called to "stand by hammocks," the men will stand close in and face the nettings. The midshipmen should be distributed from the forecastle aft, to assist in preserving order. The boatswain having reported the men up, and perfect silence being maintained, the officer of the deck will direct him to pass such orders as are necessary—such as slinging clean hammocks, boat's crew in readiness to go away (if required), &c., &c. He then directs the boatswain to pipe: *uncover;* the men stationed to pass out hammocks, then man the side and throw back the clothes; the command is then given: *pipe down.*

The men should not be allowed to *answer* when their numbers are called, but each man should step up and receive his hammock without a word; throw it over his right shoulder, take it below, and sling it. No hammocks should be thrown on the deck. After a reasonable time, the clothes are hauled over and stopped down; the midshipmen report the fact, and they are not to thrown back again, without the permission of the officer of the deck.

QUESTION. How do you lash up a hammock?

Q. What other method is there for preparing hammocks for stowing?—[dispensing with lashings.]

Q. If lashings are used, how are they prepared?

GETTING UP HAMMOCK GIRT-LINES AND CLOTHES-LINES, AND STOPPING ON HAMMOCKS, OR CLOTHES.

In stopping clothes on, the white clothes should be stopped on the starboard side; blue on the port side, and no *holidays* left. The forecastlemen stop on forward; fore and maintopmen amidships; after-guard, mizen topmen and marines, aft. Good stops should be used to prevent their being blown away.

The hammocks should be stopped on with the numbers up and out, three stops at the head, and all stopped together at the foot. The starboard watch on starboard, and port watch on port side. The midshipmen should see that the lines are properly filled.

The lines are gotten up the night before, at sunset. About twenty minutes before that time, the officer of the deck commands: *Get the clothes-lines out; stand by to lay aloft topkeepers; lay aloft, send down whips;* the lines are gotten up from below, or out of the launch, (if stowed there,) the topkeepers send down the whips, and the lines are cleared and prepared for going aloft. When the "call" is beaten, the command is given by the officer of the deck; *Man the whips; stand by to lay aloft and bring to.* At the third roll of the drum, he commands: *Trice up, lay aloft and bring to.* When the lines are brought to: *Lay down from aloft;* the top-keepers laying down at the same time.

In the morning watch, the clothes being washed, and ready

to stop on, the command is given: *Stand by to overhaul the lines down.* The lines are cleared for lowering, and, when ready, the command is given: *Pipe down.* The lines are lowered, and clothes stopped on; when all are on: *Man the whips—trice up.* The lines should be hauled well taut.

The hammock girt-lines are gotten up in the same way; except that no men are required aloft to bring them to, (as usually fitted.) In overhauling them down, and tricing them up in the morning, the same routine is observed.

Clothes should be piped down at 11.30 A. M., if dry, and the men allowed to stow them in their bags during dinner-time. Hammocks must generally be allowed a longer time to dry; they are inspected at evening quarters, put in the division bags, and stowed in the sail-room.

All hands having been called to "stand by scrubbed clothes," and reported up by the boatswain, the command is given: *Stand by to lay aloft and cast the lines adrift; lay aloft.* The lines are cast adrift, the whips cleared, and the command given: *Pipe down; lay down from aloft.* Each man takes his clothes off the lines, and folds them up; the command is then given: *Stand by to lay aloft top-keepers—lay aloft, take off whips.* When the whips are taken off and coiled away in the tops: *Lay down from aloft.*

Top-keepers should lay aloft, and come down on their respective sides.

In piping the hammocks down, the same routine is followed; except sending men aloft to cast them adrift, (which is unnecessary.)

If the awnings are spread where the clothes are to be piped down, the commands are: *Stand by to drop the awnings;* and at the command to "lay aloft and cast the lines adrift: *Man the sides, cast off the side-stops.* The lines being cast adrift, side-stops cast off, earings singled, and windsail bowlines let go, the command is given: *Pipe down;* when the earings and whips are let go, and the men lay down, and in, at the same time.

When the whips have been taken off, and lines cleared: *Stand by to haul out the awnings.* The earings are manned, and men stand ready to haul out the side stops—(all hands are required to haul them out properly): *Haul out, man the side, and haul out the side-stops; trim the wind-sails.* When done: *Lay in and down from aloft.* (The top-keepers come down as the men lay in.)

The lines are weeded, stopped up, and paid below—decks swept down, and no clothes allowed about the decks.

QUESTION. How are clothes-lines usually fitted?
Q. How are hammock girt-lines usually made?
Q. What is meant by "holidays?"
Q. Why are the hammocks stopped on with the "numbers up and out?"
Q. What is meant by "weeding" the lines?
Q. What is an "Irish pendant?"
Q. What is a windsail?
Q. You are the officer of the deck; sails loosed, hammock-clothes rolled up, awnings spread, &c. &c. &c. You observe a rain squall gathering. What will you do?
Q. In stopping white and blue clothes on the same lines, why should the white clothes be above?

TO SPREAD THE AWNINGS, &c.

The awnings being "on a stretch," to spread them, the officer of the deck commands: *Stand by to spread the awnings.* The men are sent up from below, and the command is given: *Let go the fore-and-aft tackles, cast adrift.* The awnings are cast adrift, and hauled out on a stretch again; the lacings rove, earings passed and manned, and wind-sails hauled up from below and dipped through the holes in the awnings. All being ready: *Haul out, man the side and haul out the side-stops.* The side is manned as the earings are hauled out; the side-stops passed, and ends expended, and when all are secured: *Lay in.*

In performing this evolution, the men should not be allowed to show themselves above the rail until ordered to "man the side;" except for the purpose of reeving the earings. After the side-stops are passed, they should all remain out until the order is given to "lay in."

If the awnings are not laced before hauling out, they will be laced immediately after; foot-ropes being used for the men passing the lacings to stand on. Standing *on the awnings* should never be allowed.

The men manning the side, will be careful not to tread down the hammocks.

If the officer of the deck wishes to get the awning-curtains up, he commands: *Stand by to get the curtains up;* and when they have been gotten up on deck, and stretched along: *Man the side.* The curtains are taken up by the men manning the side, and stopped to the awning-stops; when all are up: *Lay in.*

The poop and forecastle curtains (in ships having a poop and top-gallant forecastle,) will be kept at the foot of the ladder, until the order "man the side" is given. The object is, not to show a man above the pail, until the order is given to "man the side."

To take the curtains down, the commands are: *Stand by to take the curtains down—man the side—lay in;* the curtains dropping, and men laying in together.

The curtains are rolled up and taken below to the sail-room.

If the curtains are to be transferred to the other side, the command is given: *Stand by to lift over the curtains.* They are taken down and put up as described. *To furl the awnings*, the officer of the deck commands: *Stand by to furl the awnings.* The men are all sent up from below, and being ready: *Man the side and cast adrift the side-stops.* The men lay out together, cast off the stops and single the carings; when ready: *Ease away—lay in; let go the fore-and-aft tackles.* The awnings are unhooked abaft, wind-sails dipped, and lacings unrove; they are then laid on deck, rolled up smoothly, stops passed and ends expended, and the after ends hooked. All the fore-and-aft tackles being manned: *Haul out.* They are hauled out on a taut stretch together.

QUESTION. What are the "awnings?"
Q. Describe them.
Q. What is meant by housing an awning, and how is it done?
Q. What is a "crow-foot?"
Q. What is a "sharks-mouth?"
Q. What is an "euphroe?"
Q. What is a "ridge-rope," and how fitted?
Q. What is an awning-stanchion?"
Q. What is meant by "the awnings being on a stretch?"
Q. What are the "curtains?"
Q. How are the awnings hauled out to the ridge-ropes?

HOISTING AND LOWERING BOATS.

In order to hoist the boats, the command is given: *Send the boats'-crews aft to overhaul their falls down, drop the boats and haul them on.* The falls are overhauled and lead along, and the men sent aft to hoist the boats. This is generally done at sunset, and preparations should be made some minutes before. The boats should be dropped under their falls, but not hooked on until the "call" is beaten. The starboard watch man the starboard falls, the port watch, the port falls. When the "call" is beaten, the command is given: *hook on, man the falls;* at the first roll of the drum, *haul taut*, and at the third, *hoist away*. A boatswain's mate attends at each boat and pipes "belay" when the boat is up. The stoppers are then passed, falls belayed and coiled down, and plugs taken out.

To lower the boats, the command is given: *Send the boats'-crews aft to lower their boats;* and at the third roll of the drum: (if lowered when the colors are hoisted,) *lower away.* The falls are rounded up and stopped in, and ends flemished down. The boats are hauled out to the booms—two boat-keepers in each; except at meal-times, when they relieve each other.

The men are sometimes *stationed* for running all boats up together. Boats lying at the booms should hoist and haul down their flags; and spread and furl their awnings with the ship.

QUESTION. What is meant by "stopping up" the boats'-falls?
Q. What are the boats'-falls, and how are they rove?
Q. What are the "stoppers," and how fitted?
Q. What is a "thoro-put"?
Q. What are the "plugs"?
Q. What boats are allowed a 1st class frigate, and where are they carried?
Q. Who are the boat-keepers, and what is their especial duty?
Q. How is a boat moored to the boom during the day-time, (in moderate weather?)
Q. How moor a boat at night for convenience in getting alongside? (Blowing fresh?)
Q. Before firing a salute, what do with your boats?
Q. How are the boats' awnings fitted?
Q. What are the different "pipes" used by the boatswain and his mates?
Q. How are the boats "called away"?
Q. What is a "Lewis-bolt"?

MORNING AND EVENING QUARTERS.

The men are inspected at quarters in the morning, after breakfast, to see that they are properly dressed, and that all the bright-work is clean. Each man has a particular article to keep in order, and it should be ready for inspection at the usual hour. After the "Retreat" is beaten, the different divisions are exercised, as ordered.

The object of going to quarters in the evening, is to see that every man is accounted for, and that the guns are properly secured, and everything in place.

In mustering the men, the Midshipman of the division calls their numbers; to which they answer their stations at the gun *for exercise.* After each man thoroughly understands his station for exercise, it is a good plan to cause them to answer their stations or duties at other operations. For example: at evening quarters, the officer commanding the division commands: *Answer to "Casting loose;"* the Midshipman then commences with the forward gun of the division, Number 1; Number 1 replies: "Cast loose and middle breeching," &c., &c. At another time the command is given: *Answer to "Securing;"* and so on, until the men can readily answer to every station; such as "casting loose;" "securing;" "dismounting;" "shifting trucks;" "transporting;" "sponge, load and shift breeching;" "shifting pivots;" "Fire quarters;" "fitting out boats," &c., &c., &c.

By this manner of mustering, the men soon become well drilled in all their duties at the gun.

In passing orders to his division, an officer should first command: *Attention —— Division;* and then pass the order. When wishing to muster, or address any portion of his division, he should command: 1st. *Boarders to the front;* or, *Fighting boats'-crew to the front,* &c. The men step one pace to the front, close in on the centre, and toe a seam. To dismiss them the command is given: *To your quarters.*

It is usual for the Flag officer, or Captain, to inspect the ship on Sunday. The divisions having been mustered, the command is given: *Man both sides—Toe a seam.* The men form a line on either side of the deck, and stand uncovered as the inspecting officers pass along the line.

The officers should see that all the men are dressed alike, whether at morning or evening quarters; at sea or in port.

QUESTION. How are the men called to quarters in ships where there is no drummer?

SQUARING YARDS.

The boatswain having piped "square yards," the braces are thrown off of the fife-rails, and the yards are squared by the braces. The men stationed aloft to tend the lifts, &c., assemble at the foot of the Jacob's-ladders. A boat is manned, and when the boatswain reports the yards "square by the braces," the officer of the deck commands: *Stand by to lay aloft, square yardmen—lay aloft.* The boatswain then goes ahead in the boat, and squares the yards by the lifts. He sees that all rigging is hauled taut—such as the topsail and top-gallant sheets, the bowlines, halliards, &c., &c.—and pulls round the ship for the purpose. When he is satisfied that the yards are square, and rigging taut, he returns to the ship and reports the fact to the officer of the deck, who commands: *Pipe down—lay down from aloft.*

Before the boatswain commences squaring the yards by the lifts, the officer of the deck should see that all the rigging is stopped in aloft—reef tackle, pennants, top-gallant and royal lifts and braces, studding sail gear, (if rove,) &c., &c., &c., and if there is much work of the kind to be done aloft, he should send the square yardmen aloft as soon as the boatswain pipes " square yards."

The yards should be squared after any work is done which is calculated to "throw them out"—such as furling sails, hoisting out, or in, boats, &c. Nothing tends more to the general appearance of a ship than square yards, and taut gear aloft. The decks may be in the most perfect order, the hull as "neat as a pin," but the whole may be, and is, in the eye of a sailor, spoiled, by a slack bowline, or a top-gallant yard a-cockbill. The *internal* appearance of a ship is known to, comparatively, but few; while her external appearance is criticised by the crews of all the vessels in the port.

A Midshipman should accustom himself to "look aloft," and try to be able to discover the slightest neglect. If he sees anything not stopped up, and cannot *call it by name*, he should at once lay aloft and find it out.

Some officers approve of the system of squaring yards with flags, instead of allowing the boatswain to pass the word as to the condition of the yards. To make the necessary signals, three flags are required—say a red flag for the main, white for the fore, and blue for the mizen. The boatswain faces the ship and holds the flag on the side the yard requires to be topped. For lower yards he holds the flag horizontal; for topsail yards, perpendicular; for top-gallant yards, horizontal, with the other arm extended; and for royal yards, perpendicular, with the other arm extended. When the yard is square, he lowers or waves the flag.

The boatswain's mates should carefully attend to the signals, or orders of the boatswain; the chief boatswain's mate stands at the end of the jib-boom; the others in the gangways, and on the poop. The lower booms should be squared at the same time.

QUESTION. What are the "fife-rails"?
Q. *How* are the yards squared by the braces?
Q. What are the "Jacob's-ladders," and how are they fitted.
Q. Why is it necessary to send men aloft in squaring yards?

QUESTION. Suppose you were sent out to see that all the rigging was taut; what would you look at?

Q. The word is passed, "main yard to port;" which lift would you get a pull of?

Q. What is meant by, being thrown out of "kelter"?

Q. How does an officer *hail* a man aloft?

Q. Is *anybody* allowed to hail a top?

Q. How does a man on deck attract attention from the top; or *vice versa?*

Q. What is a "Timenoguy"?

TO SCRAPE THE LIGHT SPARS, &c.

The light spars require scraping occasionally, and a windy day should be selected for the purpose. It should not be done soon after tarring down, or painting; nor with the awnings spread, as the shavings are greasy. The topmen having been sent on deck, and notified as to what is to be done, the command is given: *Lay aloft, man the boom tricing-lines, trice up.* After the work is done, command: *Stand by your booms—down booms—lay down from aloft.*

In overhauling the rigging aloft, re-fitting, &c., the men should be sent aloft, and called down, together. As soon as the hands are "turned to," the command is given: *Stand by to lay aloft;* and when the working parties have assembled at the foot of the Jacob-ladders: *lay aloft.* At 7 bells the command is given: *Stand by to lay down from aloft—lay down.*

If, at any time in port, it is necessary to send the top-keepers aloft, they should all be sent together.

In tarring down the awnings should be sent below; windsails lowered and stowed away; boom cover and hammock-cloths hauled over; and decks wet and sanded down.

In re-fitting, men are disposed to let the rigging hang loosely, ropes to show below the tops and over the ship's side, &c., when there is no necessity for it; the officer of the deck should insist upon everything being kept as ship-shape as the circumstances of the case will admit.

When a ship is to be painted inside, on the spar deck, it is customary to "jag" the running rigging inside the lower rigging; in so doing, the "jags" should be of the same height above the rail, and of an equal length. In such cases, lifts, braces, &c., should be well racked to preserve the yards square, and rigging taut.

QUESTION. What precaution should be taken aloft with reference to tar-buckets, marling-spikes, &c.?

QUESTION. How do the men tar down the fore and aft stays and backstays?
Q. How prepare for rattling down the lower rigging?
Q. Suppose you wish to re-strap the lower lift and brace blocks; how will you manage it?
Q. You wish to take off a topsail lift and examine the eye?
Q. What is a "jag"?
Q. What is the distance between the ratlins?
Q. How would you manage to paint the lower masts?
Q. What spars are usually scraped and greased?
Q. What is "slush"?

AIRING BEDDING.

The bedding of the crew is occasionally hung up in the rigging to air. All hands having been called to "stand by hammocks," the word is passed to hang the bedding in the rigging, and the hammocks are "piped down." The Officer of the Deck should see that they are hung to the *standing* rigging, particularly if the ship be at sea. It is a standing rule on board ship that nothing is ever to be made fast to the *running rigging*.

In preparing a hammock for this purpose, it should be unlashed, and one turn taken round the hammock—mattrass and blankets in the middle, with the lashing. It is secured to the rigging with the other part of the lashing.

When the Officer of the Deck wishes to re-stow the hammocks, he directs the boatswain to call all "hands stand by hammocks," and after having had the word passed to the crew to lash up their hammocks and re-stow them, gives the command, *pipe down*. The hammocks are carried below, slung on their hooks, lashed up and brought up and put in the nettings.

In lashing up their hammocks, the men should not be allowed to hang them across the decks, thus stopping up the gangway. Each man should go to his proper berth, and lash his hammock up neatly.

TO GET THE LOWER BOOMS OUT.

If the lower booms are to be gotten out when the colors are hoisted, the command, *man the lower boom topping lifts and forward guys*, is given when the "call" is beaten. At the first roll of the drum command, *haul taut—top up*, and at the third roll, *walk away with the forward guys*. The boatswain on the starboard side, and the chief boatswain's mate on the port side, attend to trimming the booms.

To get them alongside—say at sunset—command, *stand by to get the lower booms alongside—man the after guys*, when the "call" is beaten. At the third roll of the drum, *walk away with the after guys.*

The boatswain and his mate attending as before. In all such evolutions, the starboard watch work on the starboard, the port watch on the port side.

QUESTION. Is it customary to get the lower-booms alongside at sunset?

Q. Suppose you have no lower booms, how would you moor a boat alongside?

Q. What is a "lazy" painter?

MAKING AND ANSWERING SIGNALS.

All signals should be answered with the answering-pennant as soon as they are made out. The Officer of the Deck reports the *numbers* to the Captain, and sends for the Signal Officer.

In "telegraphing," the cornet is hoisted at the fore, to indicate it. The signal-book contains the necessary directions in regard to the manner of making signals by day or night.

When a signal is made by the Flag-Ship, to perform any evolution, such as "loose sails," "strike top-gallant masts," &c., the movements of the Flag-Ship are followed. It is customary to make the preparatory signal a sufficient time before. After the preparations are made, each vessel should send the men down from aloft.

In loosing sails when the colors are hoisted—say at 8 A. M.—the preparatory signal is made at 7:30. The men are sent aloft to get ready, and will lay down together when it is done. Five minutes before 8, the signal is made, "loose sails;" the vessels having answered, the men are sent aloft and the "call" beaten; the other vessels following the motion of the Flag-Ship. The booms are then triced up and men sent out to loose by all the vessels together. At the third roll of the drum, the sails are dropped, and signal and answering pennants hauled down together.

All signals are made on the same principle. The Flag-Ship should never fail to give the fleet timely warning before signaling an evolution of the kind.

It is customary to make signal to the fleet also to prepare for scrubbing hammocks or clothes—the signal being made the night before in time to get the lines up at sunset.

The Flag Officer generally issues an order to the fleet as to how signals are to be made and answered. In the following evolutions, we will describe the "routine" of the Flag-Ship; it being understood that the other vessels follow the motions of the Flag-Ship and haul down their answering pennants when the signal is hauled down. This is always the moment *of execution*.

QUESTION. What are the "numbers" employed in our service?
Q. What is the "Interrogatory" pennant?
Q. What is the "Preparatory" pennant?
Q. What is the "Church" pennant?
Q. What is the "Cornet?"
Q. What is a "Distinguishing" pennant?
Q. How are the squadrons of a fleet designated?
Q. How is a signal made to a particular ship?
Q. To a squadron?
Q. How does a ship "make her number?"
Q. How does a ship indicate that she wishes a Pilot?
Q. How does a ship indicate that she wishes a tug-boat?
Q. What is meant by hoisting a flag in a "waft" [or weft]?
Q. What is the usual signal of distress?
Q. What does the "Jack" at the mizen indicate?
Q. What does the "Jack" at the main indicate?
Q. What does the "Jack" on the bows of a boat indicate?
Q. What does the "Cornet" at the fore indicate?
Q. What does a red flag at the fore, or in a boat, indicate?
Q. What are the "Repeaters?"
Q. How are signals made in a fog?
Q. How are signals made at night?
Q. What are "numerical" signals, and how are they made?
Q. What is meant by "dipping" the colors?
Q. What is a "distance-line?"
Q. What is "the private signal?"
Q. What is an "annulling signal?"
Q. What is the "guard flag?"
Q. What is meant by a ship being under "sailing orders?"
Q. What is meant by a ship being in "quarantine," and what flag does she hoist?
Q. What is meant by receiving "pratique?"
Q. What is meant by "signal distance?"
Q. What is the "telegraphic dictionary?"

TO LOOSE SAILS.

The preparatory signal having been made, as also a signal to indicate whether the sails are to be hauled out by the bowlines, or up by the buntlines, the signal to loose sails is hoisted a few minutes before the colors are to be hoisted. All hands are called to "loose sails," and the squadron having answered, the command is given: *Beat the call—aloft sail loosers;* when the men are up, *man the boom, tricing-lines—trice up—lay out and loose—man the clew-jiggers and buntlines.* When all the sails are reported ready, and 8 o'clock has been reported, command: *Stand by to let fall at the third roll—roll off;* and at the third roll, *let fall—haul up—lay in and lay down from aloft.* The signal is hauled down as the sails are let fall. The buntlines and clew-jiggers are hauled up alike. The head sails and fore and aft sails are loosed at the same time. The head sails are thrown off the booms, but the halliards are not started.

If the sails are to be hauled out by the bowlines, command: *Man the halliards, bowlines and outhauls,* after having sent the loosers up as before. At the third roll, command: *Let fall—haul out—hoist away.* The head sails are hoisted taut up, the topsails are hauled out by the bowlines, the courses dropped, the staysails hoisted, and the topsails and spanker hauled out.

If the top-gallant and royal yards are aloft, the sails are loosed as the topsails; if the yards are in the rigging, they are loosed enough to allow the wind to blow through them, when the topsails are hauled up by the buntlines, otherwise, they are let fall.

The topsail clew-lines are sometimes kept fast when the sails are hauled up by the buntlines, and some officers prefer hauling the buntlines only up square with the yards, others again haul them higher up.

The sail loosers should shift at 7 bells, and should all be dressed alike.

The boats are lowered and lower-booms gotten out at the same time, if desired.

QUESTION. How would you prepare the sails for loosing if you were sent aloft to do so? [Out by the bowlines or otherwise.]

Q. What is the object in loosing sails?

Q. When would you haul out by the bowlines?

Q. How would you station the crew for "loosing and furling?"

Q. Are the tacks and sheets usually kept hooked to the clews of the courses in port?

Q. You are ordered to get the covers on the main and mizen topsails and mainsail, give the "commands," and explain how you will do it?

Q. In "rolling off," at which roll is the bell struck?

TO FURL SAILS.

The signal to furl sails having been made and answered, and all hands called "furl sail," command: *Aloft top-gallant and royal yardmen,* and when they have reached the topmast rigging, (where they remain until the next order,) *aloft topmen;* when the topmen have reached the futtock rigging, and the top-gallant and royal yardmen, the cross-trees, *aloft lower-yardmen. Man the buntlines and clew-jiggers,* (if they have not been hauled up, if otherwise, command: *Man the bunt-jiggers—hands by the buntlines and clew-jiggers.*) The men having gotten up, command: *Lay out,* and when fairly out, *furl away.* The signal is hauled down at the same time.

When the sails are furled, *stand by the booms—lay in down-booms—lay down from aloft.*

All the men lay down except those stationed aloft to square yards. As soon as the sails are furled, the rigging should be hauled taut, and the boatswain directed to square yards. When the yards are reported square, the men are piped down from aloft.

If the sails are hauled out by the bowlines, the boatswain calls, "all hands shorten and furl sail," and the command is given: *Man the clew-jiggers, buntlines and down-hauls.* The men are sent aloft as before, and when up, *haul taut—clew up and haul down—lay out—furl away.* The sails are furled, booms lowed, &c., &c., as before.

In furling from a bowline, the halliard and bowlines are sometimes racked after being up, and out, and the running parts overhauled through the leaders, when the command is given: "Clew up and haul down," the rackings are cut.

If the top-gallant and royal yards are in the rigging, the sails are furled with the others, if there be men enough; if not, it is customary to furl them before. To do so, the officer of the deck commands: *Stand by to furl the light sails*—the men being ready—*man the rigging—furl away, lay down!*

The flying jib should be stowed when the top-gallant sails and royals are furled. In all cases the men lay out on the head booms at the order "lay out," or "man the rigging," and stow the head sails as the others are furled.

Sails are usually furled at 11:30 A. M., if day, otherwise, at 1 or 3:30 P. M.

The Officer of the Deck should always try to have his boats alongside at the time he intends furling sails. If the boats at the booms have their sails loosed, they will be furled at the same time.

If it is not desired to furl from a bowline, the signal is made "shorten sail," and all hands are called "shorten sail." The clew-jigger, buntlines, down-hauls, and brails being manned, the command is given: *Haul tout—shorten sail.*

The signal is hauled down, the topsails and courses hauled up by the buntlines and clew-jiggers, the head sails, hauled down, and the other fore and aft sails brailed up. The sails are afterwards furled as already prescribed.

When sails are loosed, the Officer of the Deck should see that the topmen do not go aloft and "steal," when sent aloft to furl, keep the men *in* until ordered *out*, and at the command "lay down from aloft," insist upon their laying down promptly, (except the square-yardmen.)

If the sails are to be reefed, the command *reef* is given instead of "furl away." The reef-tackles must be hauled out, and when as many reefs have been taken as is desired, they are overhauled, and the command given "furl away."

QUESTION. How do you furl a course?

Q. How do you furl a topsail?

Q. How do you furl a top-gallant sail?

Q. How do you stow a jib?

Q. How do you furl a spanker?

Q. What are the "covers" of the fore-and-aft sails?

Q. All hands having been called to "shorten and furl sail," state particularly the stations of the crew; commencing with the furlers of the flying-jib.

Q. On which side are the top-gallant and royal yards when in the rigging, and how are they secured and stowed there?

Q. Suppose you wish to land the main top-gallant yard on deck, in order to unbend the sail, or to make a neat furl of it, how proceed? (Yard rope not rove.)

Q. Suppose you wish to get the top-gallant and royal yards on deck, bend the sails and get them in the rigging again; what orders will you give?

Q. What is meant by furling with the "clews out," or "in?"

TO CROSS TOP-GALLANT AND ROYAL YARDS.

A ship always crosses her top-gallant and royal yards before getting under-weigh, if the weather be fine, and it is usually done when the colors are hoisted. Also, when lying in port and wishing to exercise the crew, they are sent up in the morning, and down at night.

The preparatory signal is made a half hour before the colors are to be hoisted, and the top-gallant and royal yardmen are sent aloft to overhaul the lifts and braces. As soon as it is done, they will lay down on deck. About five minutes before the time, hoist the signal and call "all hands cross top-gallant and royal yards." The men being up, and the signal answered, command: *Aloft top-gallant and royal yardmen—man the yard ropes, sway out of the chains.* The top-gallant yards are swayed until the upper yard arms are clear of the top rims, and the royal yards about half their lengths higher. (If the yards are on deck, the command is: *Sway up and down.*) When the men are up; *Beat the call—sway aloft.* As soon as the yards are reported ready. command: *Tend the braces—stand by to sway across at the third roll; roll off.* At the first roll: *Stand by;* and at the third: *Sway across.*

The signal is hauled down, and the lifts and braces immediately gotten down to the square marks. The yards are then squared, and the top-gallant and royal yardmen "piped down" with the square yardmen. If the other yards have been previously squared, the command is given: *Lay down from aloft,* as soon as the upper yards are squared.

It is a good plan to stop the yard ropes out as soon as the yards are crossed, and stradied; and then to stop the yard ropes in again to the slings with a yarn. It should be done neatly, if done at all, and *before* the yards are squared by the boatswain.

QUESTION. Give the "stations" for crossing the top-gallant and royal yards.

Q. Explain the means of crossing them.

Q. Give the duties of each man aloft.

Q. *Why* is it a good plan to stop the yard ropes out, as mentioned above?

Q. Are the yards sent up before or abaft the lower and topsail yards?

Q. Suppose you were sent aloft to "prepare" for crossing the top-gallant and royal yards; what preparations would you make?

Q. In squaring the yards by the braces after they are swayed across, which brace will require to be hauled in the most?

Q. What is meant by swaying a mast "an end?"

TO SEND DOWN THE TOP-GALLANT AND ROYAL YARDS.

About five minutes before sunset, call "all hands down top-gallant and royal yards," and hoist the signal. When answered, command: *Aloft top-gallant and royal yardmen.* If the yard ropes have not been previously stopped out, command: *Stop out the yard ropes.* When that is done, command: *Beat the call—send down the tripping lines.* (If the yard ropes are not down on deck, they are sent down with the tripping lines.) *Man the yard ropes and tripping lines; roll off.* At the first roll, *stand by;* and at the third, *sway.* The yards are lowered as rapidly as possible, and received by the topmen in the rigging, or on deck, as desired. The lifts and braces are stopped in, and hauled taut; and the command given: *Lay down from aloft.*

If the yard ropes have been stopped in to the slings with a yarn, command: *Break stops,* at the first roll of the drum.

The signal is hauled down at the command, "sway."

If the yards are to be stowed in the rigging, the topmen stationed to receive them, should lay aloft together at the third roll of the drum, and lay down together at the command, "lay down."

QUESTION. Give the "stations" for the above evolution.

Q. How would you prepare a yard for coming down?

Q. How are the lifts and braces "stopped in?"

Q. Give the duties of each man aloft.

Q. What is a "tripping line?"

Q. Why is the cautionary command, "stand by," given, in evolutions of this kind?

Q. Some ships send down top-gallant and royal yards without sending a man aloft; how is it done?

TO CROSS TOP-GALLANT AND ROYAL YARDS, AND LOOSE SAIL.

The preparatory signal having been made a half hour before the colors are to be hoisted, call all hands "cross top-gallant and royal yards, and loose sail," five minutes before the time. Send the yardmen up, and sway the yards out of the chains, and command: *Beat the call; aloft sail loosers; sway aloft.* The men are sent out to loose, and the top-gallant and royal yardmen cast off the gaskets of their sails, ready to let them fall with the others; when all ready, command: *Stand by to let fall, and sway across, at the third roll. Roll off.* At the first roll, *stand by;* and at the third, *let fall—sway across.*

The sails are hauled up by the buntlines, or out by the bowlines, as desired; and the men are sent in, and down from aloft, by the means previously given.

The sails are furled, when dry, and the yards sent down at sunset, as before directed.

Some officers prefer sending sail-loosers aloft, and giving the command: "Trice up, lay out and loose," at the order to beat the "call;" and if sending yards up at the same time, to sway them aloft when the sail-loosers "lay out;" but, unless the yards are swayed aloft and prepared for crossing very quickly, the men are kept on the yards, in waiting, too long to present a good appearance.

The routine presented above is, perhaps, the best, in most cases.

QUESTION. Give the "stations" for the above evolution.

Q. You are ordered to cross yards and haul out by the bowline; give the "commands" in succession.

TO SEND UP, AND DOWN, THE TOP-GALLANT MASTS.

If the masts are to be sent up when the colors are hoisted, make preparations, and hoist the preparatory signal a half hour before. Five minutes before the time, hoist the signal and call "all hands up top-gallant masts." When the signal has been answered, command: *Aloft topmen; man the mast ropes; sway up and down.* The masts are swayed with their heels just clear of the deck. When the topmen are up, command: *Beat the call; sway aloft.* The masts are swayed up; royal rigging placed; swayed higher, and top-gallant rigging placed, and then swayed up and fidded. They should be fidded together, if possible. The officer of the deck, waiting until the royal rigging is placed on all, and then swaying up to place the top-gallant rigging, and when that is done, swaying up and fidding. Having fidded, command: *Stand by to launch at the third roll. Roll off.* At the first roll, *stand by;* and at the third, *launch.* The mast-ropes are let go, the signal hauled down, and the masts stayed as quickly as possible. When done, command: *Lay down from aloft.*

To send them down at sunset, make the preparatory signal a half hour before; send the men aloft to make the necessary preparations, and when done, send them on deck. Five minutes before sunset, hoist the signal, and call "all hands down top-gallant masts:" *Aloft topmen; man the mast ropes.* When ready: *Beat the call; sway up and out fids; stand by to lower at the third roll. Roll off.* At the third roll, *lower away.* The masts are lowered on deck, signal hauled down, and rigging hauled taut and stopped in. Finally, commands: *Lay down from aloft.*

The flying jib-boom should be gotten out, and in, with the top-gallant masts.

The top-gallant masts may be swayed up and fidded without waiting for each other, if desired. In performing the evolution in part, however, it presents rather a better appearance to cause them to do so. The men are sometimes "stationed" for this evolution, but if not, the officer of the deck should not allow more men to lay aloft than is necessary.

When the masts are swayed up in the morning and sent down at night, it is usual to keep them up and down the lower masts, with the mast ropes wove.

QUESTION. What preparations would you make for sending up top-gallant masts?

Q. What preparations for sending out the flying jib-boom?

Q. What are the duties of the fore castlemen, fore, main and mizen topmen respectively, on deck and aloft?

Q. Explain the manner of sending up and down a top-gallant mast.

Q. Explain the manner of getting the flying jib-boom out, or in.

Q. Station the men for the above evolution.

Q. How are the mast ropes rove? [Single or double.]

Q. What is a "fid," and what a "preventor fid?" and what is a "patent fid?"

Q. Are the masts sent up before, or abaft the lower and topsail yards?

Q. How would you "stay" top-gallant masts?

Q. What preparations would you make for sending down top-gallant masts, and rigging in flying jib-boom?

Q. What are jack-blocks?

Q. After the masts are down, what is done with the rigging?

Q. How are the top-gallant masts sometimes made, so as to admit of the yard ropes and mast ropes being quickly rove, when shifting masts; or, crossing yards and sending up masts at the same time.

Q. Boyd recommends "cutting a lizard hole aslant through the mast, something more than the length of the topmast head, below the royal sheave-hole;" what is the object of it?

Q. How would you *house* top-gallant masts?

Q. Give the "commands?"

Q. The top-gallant masts are housed, and you wish to fid them when the colors are hoisted; give the "commands."

TO SEND UP TOP-GALLANT MASTS, AND CROSS TOP-GALLANT YARDS.

In performing this evolution, the masts should be fidded, the fore-and-aft stays, and the standing barkstays set up before swaying aloft the yards. The topmen should, therefore, have their luffs on, ready to get the rigging down to the old nips without delay. Unless jack blocks are used, there will be a delay in sending the yards up, unless the yard ropes are quickly rove. The ends, then, should be aloft, and as soon as the sheave appears above the cap, they should be rove, and a hauling line bent on from the deck from abaft. Some hands having been previously stationed for the purpose, man the hauling line and reeve the yard rope. The men at the mast ropes turn round to the yard ropes, as soon as the masts are fidded. The standing parts of the yard ropes are hooked to the slings of the yards in readiness, before the evolution.

If the masts and yards are to be sent up when the colors are hoisted, make signal as before, and call "all hands up top-gallant masts and top-gallant yards." Send the men aloft; beat the call; sway up; fid top-gallant masts; then sway aloft the yards, and cross at the third roll—the signal being hauled down at the same time.

The royal yards may be crossed with the others, if desired.

QUESTION. Station the men for the above evolution.

Q. Give the "commands" in succession.

Q. What preparations are necessary?

TO SEND DOWN TOP-GALLANT MASTS, AND YARDS.

Unless jack blocks are used in this evolution, the yards must be sent down, before the masts can be lowered lower than the sheaves in the top-gallant mast heads. A few hands should be stationed to round down on the standing parts of the yard ropes, as soon as the yards are on deck, and when the end approaches the sheave hole, the men aloft unreeve it, and keep it at the topmast head.

Having made preparations, make the signal, and call "all hands down top-gallant masts and yards" five or ten minutes before sunset, [supposing that the evolution is to be performed at that time.] Send the men aloft; beat the call; sway up and out fids, as before. At the third roll, sway and lower away. Lower the yards on deck, and the top-gallant masts as far as the sheaves. As soon as the yard ropes are unrove, lower away the masts.

Haul down the signal at the third roll.

The evolution cannot be made a successful one, unless *marks* have been previously put on the mast ropes and yard ropes, and careful hands stationed at them to lower, &c.

There should be no "singing out" from aloft.

If jack blocks are used, sway the yards at the third roll, and lower away all together.

QUESTION. What preparations are necessary?
Q. Station the men.
Q. Give the "commands" in succession.
Q. How are jack blocks fitted, if used?
Q. What is the difference between "striking" and "housing" top-gallant masts?

TO SEND UP TOP-GALLANT MASTS, AND LOOSE SAILS.

Having made preparations, make the signal, and call "all hands up top-gallant masts and loose sails at five minutes before the colors are to be hoisted. Beat the call, sway aloft, and send the sail loosers aloft together, (having previously sent the topmen up to receive the masts.) At the third roll, launch and let fall, hauling up the buntlines, &c., as before described.

The sails are furled when dry, and the masts sent down at sunset. The words of command in sending the masts up, and loosing, would be, in succession: *Man the yard ropes; aloft topmen; sway "up and down."* Beat the call; *sway aloft; aloft, sail loosers. Man the boom tricing lines; trice up; lay out; loose.; man the clew jiggers and buntlines,* (or other necessary gear, if to haul out by the bowlines.) *Stand by to launch and let fall at the third roll. Roll off; stand by; launch; let fall; haul up, lay in;* and when the masts are stayed and rigging set up: *lay down from aloft.*

The loosers of the courses and fore-and-aft sails lay down as soon as the sails are loosed.

TO SEND UP TOP-GALLANT MASTS AND YARDS, AND LOOSE SAILS.

In performing this evolution, the same routine is observed. The yards are crossed and sails loosed at the third roll.

QUESTION. What preparations are necessary?
Q. Give the "commands," in succession.

TO MEND SAILS.

"Mending sails" is furling them afresh. To do this properly, the sails should be let fall, the buntlines hauled up, and the leeches, &c., passed in afresh. The clewlines are not started. Having made signal five minutes before, and called "all hands mend sails," beat the call, and send the men aloft, as in furling sails. When the men are up to the yards, command: *trice up, lay out and loose; man the buntlines; roll off.* At the third roll: *let fall—haul up.* When the men are ready: *Furl away; stand by the booms; lay in; down booms; lay down from aloft.* Haul taut the gear, square yards, &c., &c., as in "furling sails."

What is the object in mending sails?

HOISTING IN AND OUT BOATS.

Having directed the boatswain to call "all hands out boats," the order is given to *clear away the boats*, and, the topmen being ready: *Aloft topmen.* The boom-cover is thrown back, and everything not belonging to the boats thrown out and laid in the gangways, and the yard and stay tackles prepared for going aloft. The men aloft overhaul the burtons and prepare the whips, and when ready: *Lay out—send down whips—hook the burtons.* As soon as the whips are sent down, the yard tackles and triatic stay are bent on. *Man the whips and port fore brace—trice up—brace in the fore yard.* As soon as the yard is braced in, and tackles hooked, haul taut the lifts, braces, burtons, trusses and rolling tackles, and "hook on" the upper boat. *Man the stays, haul taut, walk away.* When the boat is high enough: *Turn with the stays, man the yards, walk away—*

3

case away the stays; and when the boat is clear of the ship's rail: *Turn with the yards—lower away.* The boat is lowered in the water, the tackles unhooked and rounded up. The launch is hoisted out in the same manner.

To send down the tackles, command: *Lay out—unhook tackles and burtons—man the starboard fore brace.* When ready: *Lower away—square the fore yard—take off the whips.* The tackles and triatic stay are lowered, made up and stowed away; the burtons rounded up and whips coiled away in the tops. As soon as the work aloft is done: *Lay down from aloft.*

The booms are now re-stowed, rigging flemished down, decks swept and yards squared.

The boats are hoisted in by similar means and orders.

What yard tackles are used for hoisting out and in boats?
When are the burtons hooked?
How are they rove?
How and where are the whips put on?
What is the triatic stay, and how fitted?
How bend on the whips for tricing up and hooking the tackles?
How many men are hoisted out in the boats?
How are the boats stowed?
Why are the burtons hooked?
How do you secure the yards?
Why is the fore yard braced in?
Is the main yard braced?
What is a winding tackle?
What precautionary command would you give before bracing fore yard?
What is stowed in the boats?
On which side is the boat supposed to be hoisted out in the above article?
Give the commands for taking in the launch, and the entire routine.
How would you divide the men at the falls?
Does the main yard require as much support in hoisting out a launch as in taking in a 32-pdr. gun of 63 cwt.?
What is about the weight of a frigate's launch?
How would you hoist out a boat at sea?
What is the windlass, usually put in our launches, to be used for?
How are the boats secured for sea?

BENDING AND UNBENDING SAILS.

Before calling "all hands to bend sails," the men are sent aloft to prepare for the evolutions—yard whips put on, gear overhauled, jib stay unrove, gaffs lowered, (if necessary,) &c., and the sails gotten up and stretched along the deck. When everything is prepared, and men sent down from aloft, the Boatswain is directed to "call all hands bend sails"—*Man the sail burtons—Aloft topmen—Sway aloft the topsails.* The topsails are swayed up to the yards, and the men aloft bend the gear. The jib stay is rove through the hanks and marrying line manned, the gear of the courses bent and manned, and the spanker bent to the gaff, and throat and peak halliards manned. When all ready: *Aloft lower yardmen—trice up the booms—haul taut—sway up and haul out—lay out and bring to.* The jib stay is run out, gaffs hoisted, and square sails hauled out together. As soon as the sails are bent, command: *Lay in—down from aloft;* unless it is intended to furl.

The yard whips are taken off, jib stay set up, &c.

To unbend sails, direct the Boatswain to call "all hands unbend sails"—*Aloft topmen—Aloft lower yardmen—man the boom tricing lines—trice up—lay out and unbend.* The men lay out on the jib-boom at the same time, and prepare the jib for coming in. The halliards and jib downhaul are manned, the gear of topsails and coursers tended, and hands by the gaff halliards. When the men aloft are ready—earings singled, &c.—*Ease away—lower away.* The jib comes in and gaffs down as the square sails are lowered. The men aloft make up the gaskets, &c. *Lay in—down booms—lay down from aloft.* The jib stay is set up again, gaffs hoisted, sails made up and stowed in the sail-room, rigging hauled taut, decks swept, &c.

How do you make up a jib?
How make up a course?
How make up a topsail?
How make up a spanker?
Bend and unbend a jib, a topsail, a course and a spanker.
What is a marrying line?
Suppose a jib is laced, how bend it?
What are the sail burtons, and where are they hooked in bending and unbending the topsails?
How is the fall of the sail burton rove?
What is a roband? and how passed?
Why are the topsails swayed aloft first?

What gear would you man *best* in swaying up a course?
Where are the yard whips hooked?
How bend a spanker which travels on the gaff?
Name the different parts of a sail.
How tell a foresail from a mainsail?
How tell the top of a sail from the bottom? the forward from the after side?
How are the top-gallant sails, royals and flying jib bent?
Mention all the gear of a jib, topsail, course and jib.
You are in charge of the deck, and are ordered to shift the main topsail—give the commands in succession..
How are studding sails bent, and where are they kept?
You are in charge of the deck, and are ordered to reeve studding gear and get the top-gallant studding sails in the tops—give the commands in succession.
The top-gallant yards are crossed, and you are ordered to unbend the main top-gallant sail—how would you do it?
The royal yards are across and you wish to unbend the main royal—how would you do it?

BOAT SERVICE.

The officer of the deck wishing to send away a boat, directs the bugler, or Boatswain's mate, to "call her away." The Midshipman of the quarter deck sees the boat manned, and calls one of the Midshipmen of the "boat duty," or "relief," to go in her. The Midshipman called makes his appearance, neatly dressed in uniform and with his side arms, and reports to the officer of the deck for orders; having received them, he gets in the boat and commands: *Up oars—shove off—let fall—give way*. If he wishes to turn the boat—say, to starboard—he commands: *Back your starboard oars—give way your port oars*.

After having shoved off, he should see that the fenders are taken in and that the painter is not trailing overboard. The bowmen should, after having shoved the boat off, resume their seats, get up their oars and let them fall together, without orders.

In pulling ashore, attention must be paid to the set of the tide.

Meeting another boat, and wishing to salute, command: *Stand by to lay on your oars*—(or, *toss your oars*, as the case may be): *Oars*, (or *Toss*,) and having passed, *Give way*. Upon approaching your place of destination, command: *In bows—way enough*. At the command "in bows," the bowmen take one stroke and toss their oars; they should then stand upright in the bows of the boat, with their boat-hooks held in both hands and heels resting on the thwart. At the command, "Way enough," the men take one stroke and toss. The starboard stroke oarsman should throw up his right arm just before tossing, as a signal. The fenders are thrown out as soon as the oars are boated.

When a Midshipman goes alongside his own, or any other ship, he should report at once to the officer of the deck.

How are the commands: "lay on your oars," "toss your oars," "trail oars," "boat your oars," and "lock your oars," executed?

What is feathering an oar?

Name the different parts of an oar.

How would you muffle an oar?

What salutes are to be observed by boats passing? [Navy Regulations.]

If a junior overtakes his superior officer, should he pass him?

Do launches or heavily laden boats salute?

How would you salute a Commodore, your boat being under sail?

You are in a boat under sail—say, two lugs, jib and jigger—it comes on to blow; how would you shorten sail?

How heave a boat to, in moderate weather? in a gale?

How tack a boat?

How wear?

How is a lug sail dipped?

How land in a surf?

How cross a bar?

How is a boat fitted out for distant service? [Ordnance Manual.]

When a boat comes alongside, what salute do the boat-keepers pay?

How do you weigh an anchor with the launch?

MILITARY HONORS AND CEREMONIES.

The Navy Regulations say, that "when the President of the Confederate States shall visit a vessel of the Navy, he shall be received upon the deck by all the officers, in full uniform; the yards shall be manned; the full guard shall be paraded, and shall present arms; the music shall give three ruffles of the drum and play a march, and a salute of twenty-one guns shall be fired. And the same honors shall be paid when he leaves the ship,"—also, the Confederate Ensign shall be displayed at the main.

Having been notified of the intended visit, the officer of the deck will get the life lines on the yards, (sending the men aloft, together, for that purpose,) and have them stopped down to the eyes of the lifts. He should assure himself that they are securely bent, or hitched, to the lifts, and prepared for hauling out, as the lives of the men depend upon it. It is usual to select and station the men for the different yards.

The Signal Quartermaster has the ensign bent on and stations men at the halliards. The Executive officer gives the orders about officers being in full dress, the guard and music, and also the salute.

When the boat containing the President heaves in sight, the officer of the deck will drop the boats, notify the Commanding and Executive officers, direct the Boatswain to "call all hands man yards," call the officers, turn out the guard, and have the side tended by the Boatswain and eight side boys. He should notify the men, before sending them aloft, that they are to lay out at the first gun and in at the last, and that those on the mizen yards are to face forward; the others aft; also, that the life lines are *not* to be taken off. Just before the boat gets alongside: *Aloft top-gallant yardmen—aloft topmen—Aloft lower yardmen.* If the head and spanker booms are to be manned, the men stand in readiness to lay out with the yardmen. The ensign is rounded up, and the Quartermaster directed to break the stops at the first gun, and to haul down the pendant. The men aloft must keep close in to the slings of the yard.

As the President is "piped over," the drums roll, marines present arms, and music plays. As soon as the boat drops astern, the Executive officer commences firing the salute. At the first gun: *Lay out—break stops*, and at the last: *Lay in—lay down from aloft.*

When the President leaves, the officers are called, guard turned out, side tended, &c. The officer in charge of the boat should be directed to pull ahead of the ship. The men are sent aloft with directions to face forward, after the boat has shoved off. When the boat is clear of the ship, the salute is fired. At the first gun: *Lay out,* and at the last: *Lay in—off life lines—lay down from aloft.* The ensign is hauled down and stops of pendant broken at the last gun.

Haul up the boats, square the lower booms (if they have been topped up,) &c., &c.

The officer in command of the boat (a Lieutenant) will lay on his oars while the salute is being fired. In taking off the life lines, the men stationed for so doing must be cautioned not to "start anything" until the men are off the yards. After the salute is fired, the Marine officer is directed to "dismiss the guard."

How are the "life lines" gotten on the yards?

How instruct the men to stand securely on the yards?
How is a salute fired?
What precautions are to be taken before firing? [Ordnance Manual.]
Why "stop the life lines down to the eyes of the lifts"?
How is the Vice President received? an ex-President? an ex-Vice President? a Foreign Sovereign? a Cabinet Officer? a Judge of the Supreme Court? a Governor? a Flag Officer? a Captain? a Commander? a Lieutenant Commanding? a Lieutenant? a Warrant Officer?
What is the salute of an Admiral? a port Admiral? a Flag Officer? a Captain? a Commander? persons of diplomatic rank? [Navy Regulations, pages 32 *et seq.*]
What powder and what charge of powder, is to be used in saluting?
How is the absence of a Flag Officer, or a Commanding Officer indicated at night?
What are the Ceremonies to be observed at the Gangway? [Navy Reg., p. 45.]
Is it usual to keep the marines on deck in port?
How would you prepare for a salute—say, to an English Consul?
You are in company with an English fleet, on the Queen's birthday; what flags would you hoist?
How is a ship dressed?
You being in charge of the deck, how and when would you hoist and haul down the flags in dressing ship?
What is the general definition of a "life line"?
You are "cheered" by a passing vessel and wish to return it; give the orders.
When is it usual to "cheer ship"?
How are officers received at night?
You are in charge of a boat containing an officer, who is "cheered," what will you do?
What is the order about the hour of hoisting the colors and beating the tattoo?
Would you ever use a National Ensign for dressing a ladder?

HOISTING IN PROVISIONS, WATER, &c.

The launch being nearly alongside, with a load of provisions, call all hands "clear launch"—*Aloft top-keepers*—(of the Main top only)—*Send down whips.* The water whip and stay are bent on, and a burton hooked to support main yard if necessary. *Man the whips—Starboard main brace—trice up—brace up main yard.* The yard and stay tackles are triced up and hooked, and the main yard braced a little up and secured. A mat is placed in the gangway to land the barrels, which are to be landed and struck down the fore hatch; the fife is in readiness to play; the Pay Master's Steward to take an account of the provisions received; a tarpaulin is put over the port-hammock nettings for the Boatswain's mate to stand on while attending to the discharging the boat; the Mate of the hold is notified to prepare to receive provisions; and the mates of the lower decks have hanging mats hung in the hatches, and men stationed to guide the barrels, &c., down clear, ladders unshipped, &c.; the forecastlemen go in the boat to sling provisions, the foretopmen tend in the port gangway to roll the barrels forward, placing mats in the gangway to prevent soiling the deck; the maintopmen man the stay, the afterguard and mizentopmen the yard tackle; the mainmastmen unhook the tackles when the barrels are landed. The Master's Mate of the forecastle superintends the whole.

As each barrel (or barrels) is hooked on, the Officer of the deck commands: *Haul taut—walk away with the yard—haul over the stay—lower away—round up and hook on.*

When the launch is cleared, if it is not intended to send down the "yard and stay," they are hooked to an eyebolt in the main channels and hauled taut; otherwise command: *Aloft, and stand by to send down the yard and stay—lay out and unhook—*(taking off burton at the same time)—*man the port main brace;* when ready: *Lower away—square the main yard. Take off the whips.* As soon as the whips are coiled away: *Lay down from aloft.*

After all work the rigging is flemished down and decks swept. *This rule is general.*

Where is the yard tackle hooked?
Where is the "stay" hooked?
What is the water whip?
Why is the main yard braced a little up?
What provisions are stowed forward?
How would you strike barrels down the fore hatch?
What is a "beef" tackle?
How do you sling a barrel?
What is the weight of a barrel of bread?
Where and how is bread stowed?
How is the bread-room lined?
How cleaned to receive new bread?
Would you stow good and bad bread in the same bread-room, in bulk?

What is the weight of a barrel of beef or pork?
Where is it stowed?
Where is whiskey stowed? molasses? vinegar? beans? rice? flour? sugar? coffee? tea? butter? cheese? oil? paints? candles? Boatswain's stores? Gunner's stores? Master's stores? Pay-Master's stores? Carpenter's stores? Sail-Maker's stores? Surgeon's stores? Mess stores?
What is the difference between "wet and dry provisions"?
How do you "start" whiskey?
What arrangements make and precautions adopt?
In starting molasses, vinegar and whiskey through the same hose, which would you start first? and which last?
What is meant by "making a bull" of a barrel?
How do you rig a "starting tub"?
How is water taken aboard?
Where is it put?
What is the allowance of water, per man, a day?
What is a scuttle-butt?
Why is a sentry stationed there?
How would you raft off water casks?
How is wood taken in, and where stowed?
Why are the sticks counted?
Why is the wood barked?
Why do you bark the hoops of beef and pork barrels before stowing?
How is sand taken in, and where stowed?
How is coal taken in, and where stowed?
What preparations make for coaling ship?
What do you do with the boats while coaling?
How do you stow the hold?
How stow the spirit-room?

SERVING OUT PROVISIONS, CLOTHING, SMALL STORES, &c. INSTRUCTIONS ON

What is the call for serving out provisions?
Who attends?
What does the Navy Ration consist of?
If the crew wish to complain of any part of the ration, how should they do it?
If the Pay-Master receives bad bread or beef, what does he do?
What is a "harness cask," and what is it used for?
How is the ration cooked?
How is a galley inspected?

Who is the Jack of the Dust?
Who is the Loblolly boy?
Who is the Jemmy Ducks?
How are the small stores issued?
What are called small stores?
What are the Mess Bills, and who makes them out?
Why should an officer attend at all issues to the men?
What are clothes' lists and Requisitions?
What is the object of making out clothes' lists?
What is the duty of an officer commanding a division, in relation to the clothing of his men?
How often are clothes' lists and requisitions made out?
How is clothing issued?
Who attends?
What are "Slops"?

Part III.

EVOLUTIONS.

Note—The Student must be prepared to illustrate every evolution by a Diagram.

TACKING.

1. BY THE WIND ON STARBOARD TACK, UNDER ALL PLAIN SAIL, (VIZ: ROYALS AND FLYING JIB, MAINSAIL AND SPANKER,) TACK SHIP; MODERATE BREEZE AND SMOOTH SEA.

The officer of the deck commands: (1.) *Ready about.*

At this command the men repair to their stations, as assigned them by the Station Bill. The Mate of the forecastle sees hands by the head sheets and bowlines, by the fore tack and sheet, men on head booms to light over sheets, lee fore tack and weather sheet stretched along, hands to let go and overhaul fore lifts trusses and rolling tackles—also, to overhaul and set up breast backstays, hands aloft to bear abaft and abreast backstays, and to overhaul lifts and trusses aloft, both fore clew gaskets manned, also lee main tack, and finally, hands by main tack and all the main-bowlines.

The Midshipman of the quarter-deck will see weather main and lee cross-jack braces, main clew garnets and weather main sheet manned, hands by lee main braces, main sheet, and weather cross-jack braces and bowlines; at mainmast, to overhaul main lifts, trusses and rolling tackles, and tend head braces; hands to overhaul and set up main and mizen topmast breast backstays, weather spanker sheet manned, and lee one and vangs tended, also the topping lifts; and finally, men aloft to bear abaft and abreast backstays, and overhaul lifts and trusses.

The men being at their stations, the officer of the deck commands: (2.) *Ready, ready,* and directs the helmsman to ease down the helm, at the same time hauling the spanker boom amidships; when the helm is down, he commands: (3.) *Helm's a-lee,* on which the head sheets are let go and overhauled; when the wind is well out of the mainsail, (4.) *Rise tacks and sheets,* (keeping fast fore tack,) and immediately after, (5.) *Overhaul lifts and trusses—bear abaft breast backstays;* the main tack and sheet being raised, the lee main tack is shortened in; when the wind is ahead, or a point on the weather bow [observing that the weather lerch of the main topsail is *well* aback; or at night, waiting for the spanker to flap.] (6.) *Haul well taut—Mainsail haul;* the after yards are swung, main tack got down, yards braced up and sheet hauled aft. Now shift over head sheets, rise fore tack, pull up weather spanker boom topping lift and bear boom over to leeward. (7.) *Head Braces;* the Mate of forecastle will man fore tack and sheet and head bowlines, and haul aft head sheets; when the aft sails are nearly full, (8.) *Haul taut—Let go and haul.* The head yards are braced sharp up and tack got down. Right the helm when she has fallen off sufficiently far, or a little before, (supposing her to have kept her headway.) If she gathers sternboard while in stays, right the helm and shift it over.

Finally, get the tacks well down, brace up sharp, trim all the sheets, haul taut weather braces, lifts, trusses and rolling tackles, set up backstays, haul the bowlines and coil down the rigging.

QUESTION. Suppose you are hauling the head yards rather late, and the ship is well off the wind on the other or new tack; how proceed?

Q. You are hauling the head yards too soon, and the ship flies to; how proceed?

Illustrate the Evolution by a Diagram.

2. UNDER ALL PLAIN SAIL ON STARBOARD TACK, TACK SHIP; THE WIND BEING VERY LIGHT AND SHIP'S STAYING DOUBTFUL.

In this case the ship will lose her headway, and must be tacked with sternboard. Man the head downhauls and proceed as before, except that as the helm is put down, the lee head braces will be checked and bowlines let go—bracing the topsail and upper yards a little in. At the order, *Helm's a-lee,* haul down head sails; brace up the head yards again as she comes to. Haul mainsail when the wind is a *little* on the *lee* bow, and as she will now probably lose her headway, right the helm, and shift it over as she gathers sternboard. Hoist head sails, and keep the weather sheets aft, afterwards proceed as before.

Note.—If it is probable that the ship will *not* lose her headway, do not check the lee head braces; nor trim aft the weather head sheets after hoisting them again, unless she is absolutely going astern *at* that *time.*

QUESTION. Having raised tacks and sheets, she falls off again; how proceed for another trial?
Q. Why does a ship generally carry a slack or lee helm as the wind falls light?
Q. Why does she carry it more a-weather as the wind freshens?
Explain the action of the rudder.

3. TO TACK; UNDER DOUBLE REEFED TOPSAILS, COURSES AND JIB—(SEA ON WEATHER BOW.)

Proceed as in the preceding case. The helm must be righted the *moment* the headway ceases to avoid injury to the rudder pintles; if there be much sea, do not put it more than half down in sternboard, and caution the men at the wheel to "hold hard" while doing so. Set the spanker before putting the helm down, and do not check the lee head braces if there is any probability of her preserving her headway long enough not to require it.

QUESTION. Having swung the main yard in stays, she refuses to go either way, or is "in irons;" how proceed?
Q. Why not shorten in lee fore tack as well as the main?
Q. Why does the ship heel more when the sails first fill, after stays?
Q. In tacking, a lee top-gallant brace jambs; what do?

WEARING.

4. BY THE WIND ON STARBOARD TACK, UNDER ALL PLAIN SAIL. WEAR SHIP—WIND VERY LIGHT.

The officer of the deck commands: *Stand by to wear ship—Man the main clew-garnets and buntlines—Spanker brails.* The stations of the men are pretty much the same as in tacking. The Mate of the forecastle will man the main buntlines with the hands stationed at the lee main tack and fore clew-garnets. The quarter-deck Midshipman will assist the men at the main clew-garnets and spanker brails, with hands from the main and cross-jack braces, (the latter returning to their stations after the mainsail and spanker are in.) When manned; *Haul taut—up mainsail—clear away the outhaul—brail up.* (It is not necessary to haul up the leechlines.) The man at the wheel having been directed to put the helm up: *Clear away the after bowlines—brace in.* The after yards are braced in as the ship falls off, keeping the mizen topsail shivering, but the *main just fall.* As the yards come in, the lifts and trusses are attended to, and the lee breast backstays breasted. The after yards should be square by the time the ship has brought the wind on the quarter. when the officer of the deck will command: *Head Braces*—and the braces being manned: *Rise fore tack and sheet—Clear away the head bowlines—square the head yards.* The fore lifts and trusses will be attended to, and lee backstays breasted as the yards come in. The head sheets will now be shifted over, port fore tack and starboard sheet led along. The spanker boom will be borne over on the starboard quarter and outhaul led out. The port main tack and starboard sheet led along. *Main braces—brace up,* as the wind draws on the port quarter. *Man main tack and sheet—spanker outhaul, clear away the rigging—haul aboard—let go the brails—haul out.* Brace up after yards and trim all sharp. Haul down flying-jib, and brail up jib, if necessary, to bring her to. When the wind is on the port beam: *Head braces, brace up head yards—haul forward fore tack and head bowlines.* Trim sharp forward and meet her with the helm and head sheets. Haul taut lifts, &c., and coil down rigging.

The starboard breast backstays are borne abaft as the yards are braced up.

QUESTION. Give the stations of the men in wearing.

Q. Why is the main topsail kept *full?*

Q. Suppose you were stationed at the mainmast, what directions would you give in reference to the hauling taut, or overhauling of lifts and trusses?

Illustrate the Evolution by a Diagram.

5. TO WEAR UNDER CLOSE REEFED MAIN TOPSAIL, FORE, MAIN AND MIZEN STORM STAYSAILS. (GALE.)

All hands being called to wear ship, see the main and mizen storm staysail downhauls, weather main and lee cross-jack braces manned—and lifts, trusses, rolling tackles and preventer braces, manned and tended. In a small ship, it may be as well to batten down if the sea should be very heavy. Everything being ready, the officer of the deck will wait for a smooth time, and as the *ship is falling off,* haul down the mizen storm staysail, *start the weather main braces,* and put the helm up. The cross-jack yards will be kept pointed to the wind, but the main topsail will, *on no account,* be lifted. As the ship falls off, continue to brace so as to have the after yards square by the time the wind is on the quarter. Haul down main storm staysail and shift over the sheet, as well as that of the mizen storm staysail. *Right the helm* in time to prevent her coming to on the other tack before you are *prepared for it.* As the after yards are braced in the lifts, trusses, &c., must be very carefully attended to. Now brace round the head yards on the other tack, using same precautions, and being particular to *ease them up*, and if the fore storm staysail is not fitted with two sheets, haul it down. shift over the sheet, hoist it again, and haul aft the sheet. Man main and cross-jack braces, main and mizen storm staysail halliards. Wait for a smooth time, ease down the helm, brace up and hoist mizen storm staysail, and as the wind gets well on the quarter, hoist main storm staysail. *Meet her in time.* Do not brace the yards too sharp, and be careful in tending the weather braces.

See everything snug and pipe down.

Note.—If there should be a very heavy sea running, it would be well to set the foresail, either whole or goose-winged—hauling it up and furling it when before the wind.

QUESTION. Why *start* the weather main brace *just before* putting the helm up?

Q. Why not shiver the main topsail?

Q. What is meant by goose-winging a foresail, and how is it done?

Q. How are the preventer fore and main and topsail braces rove?

Q. What is meant by "waiting for a smooth time"?

Q. What is meant by "as she falls off"?

Q. What is to be apprehended in wearing in a heavy gale?

Q. Suppose that after having gotten the wind on the quarter, after yards square and just about to brace the head ones, the sea striking you on the quarter, throws you round up in the wind on the same tack as before, how proceed?

Q. Give the stations of the men, and state exactly how the lifts, &c., should be attended.

Q. Wear ship—being hove to under close reefed main topsail and main trysail.

6. WEAR SHIP IN A STRONG BREEZE.

In a strong breeze, under double reefs and courses, a ship will sometimes miss stays and render it necessary to wear. Or. the evolution may be preferred to tacking, on account of the great strain brought on the masts when the sails are aback, and the risk of carrying away rudder in case of rapid sternway; or it may be to save wear and tear of sails. Sometimes, too, when lying "off and on" a port, waiting for daylight, to enter. the ship being under topsails and foresail, the officer of the deck may choose to wear instead of setting the mainsail and tacking. In any of these cases, proceed as in Article 4, *except* that the main topsail may be *shivered* at once, observing to *start* the weather braces before putting the helm up. Brace the after yards square and commence squaring the head yards by the time the wind is on the quarter, so as not to be obliged to *right* the helm when before the wind. Brace up aft and then forward, as in Article 4, *easing* the yards up as in Article 5. Right the helm in time as she comes to.

Haul everything taut and coil down rigging.

Note.—In wearing with the watch in a strong breeze, if there is a probability of the ship *flying to very rapidly*, either from the known qualities of the ship, or the state of the sea, the head yards may be braced round *on the other tack* when before the wind. It must be observed, however, that more distance will be lost *to leeward* than if they had been left square and braced up after the wind was *on the beam on the other tack*.

In wearing *together*, in fleet sailing, the order would be thrown into *disorder*, if the vessels adopted different methods of performing the evolution; the *proper method is* to perform *all evolutions as quickly* as consistent with the safety of the ship.

The spanker and mainsail can be used at the discretion of the officer of the deck in the above case. The ship is supposed to have *good headway*.

QUESTION. In what does the last case differ from Article 4?

Q. What is the objection, if any, to bracing the after yards round *in the other tack*, as soon as the wind is aft—at the same time letting go lee head braces and bowlines; as in Murphy's Seamanship, page 20, Evolutions?

Q. Under double-reefed topsails, courses, jib and spanker, (starboard tack,) wear ship—giving the stations of the men and *words of command.*

Q. Same case: In bracing up the after yards on the new tack, (head yards being square,) she *flies to suddenly*, brings the head yards aback, and commences going astern; how proceed? Give the words of command in succession.

7. BOX-HAULING.

In cases where there is not room enough to leeward to wear, or where we wish to go round without fore-reaching much to windward, recourse is had to Box-hauling.

The officer of the deck commands: *Ready about.* The men repair to their stations as in tacking, except that the main clew-garnets and buntlines, spanker brails and weather head braces are manned in addition.

All being ready, the command *Helms-a-lee* is given, as soon as the helm is ordered to be put down; all the head sheets are let go and overhauled. When the wind is out of the mainsail: *Haul taut—rise tacks and sheets—up mainsail and spanker—brace abox the head yards, square away the after yards.* As she will now get stern board, keep the helm as it is, and haul aft the weather jib sheets. When she has fallen off sufficiently to fill the after sails, and begins to gather way, right the helm and put it the other way.

Brace up the after yards, set spanker and mainsail, as the wind gets on the quarter: flow the head sheets, and, if necessary, square the head yards, to let her come to. Meet her with the helm, head sheets, and braces, if necessary.

QUESTION. By the wind on the port tack, under all plain sail, land discovered ahead and on both bows—*close aboard.* What do?

Q. By the wind under top-gallant sails, courses, jib and spanker, wind freshens and ship commences to gripe. What do?

Q. What causes a ship to gripe?

Q. By the wind under all plain sail, on starboard tack. Wind from N. E.—it suddenly shifts to S. S. W. How proceed, supposing your course to be N. by E.?

Under same circumstances, wind shifts to East? Ship's course as given by the Captain. Why?

8. CHAPELLING.

When a ship is taken aback by a change of wind, or by her coming to against the helm, if it be required to bring her by the wind on same tack, the evolution is called *chapelling.* The better plan to pursue in this case is to put the helm for stern board, keep aft the weather head sheets, up mainsail and spanker, and square the after yards; afterwards, proceed as in *box-hauling.*

If there is anything to prevent you from using the men, the evolution may be performed by the use of the helm, head and spanker sheets alone.

Much time will elapse before the ship is by the wind again on the tack required.

This method should not be adopted, unless in very light airs, the ship should be caught aback during Divine service, or in case of sickness among the crew rendering it advisable not to disturb them.

QUESTION. By the wind on starboard tack, under all plain sail, taken aback; recover her by same tack on the first method. Give all the orders.

Q. Same case. State particularly how you would perform the manœuvre, using the helm, spanker and jib sheets alone.

Q. How do you trim the yards on the wind? Suppose the wind freshens?

Q. In beating to windward, what proportion does the distance gained to windward bear to the whole distance sailed? How calculate it? (Supposing the ship to sail within six points of the wind, and to make no lee way.)

Q. By the wind, under all sail, on the front tack, wind shifts to about one point on the port bow; recover the ship on the same tack. Give the necessary orders.

9. TAKEN ABACK.

BY THE WIND ON STARBOARD TACK, WIND SHIFTS TO PORT BOW.

As she will now lie her course on the other tack, the officer of the deck commands: *Ready about*, in order to bring the men to their stations, and proceeds as in tacking.

QUESTION. Give the orders, and describe the above evolution.

Q. Tacking in a light breeze, all sail set, the ship comes nearly head to wind, loses her headway, and commences to fall off again; you are ordered to get her round on the other tack *in the quickest manner possible.* Give the orders in succession.

Q. Illustrate the above evolutions by diagrams.

Q. By the wind on port tack, all sail set, ship comes to against the helm. What do?

WIND HAULING AFT.

10. BY THE WIND ON STARBOARD TACK, UNDER ALL SAIL, WIND HAULS AFT GRADUALLY.

The officer of the deck perceiving that the wind has hauled a little aft, (the ship heading her course,) will ease a little of the head and spanker sheets; also, the fore and main sheets; get a pull of the weather top-gallant and royal braces, check the bowlines fore and aft, and command: *Stand by to set the top-gallant studding sails.* The men aloft will put jiggers on the weather top-gallant lifts, and haul them taut, bend the halliards, man the tack, get the boom ready for going out, and man the out-jigger. If the top-gallant sail is not steadied by the bowline, the officer of the deck will steady it, and also see that the weather top-gallant clewline is steadied taut and belayed, for the man on the yard to hold on by, if necessary. The halliards being manned on deck, the command is given: *Haul taut—rig out and hoist away.* The boom is rigged out, stops cut by the man on the topsail yard, the tack hauled out, sail hoisted taut up, and sheet trimmed down. The men aloft get the boom ready for coming in, after securing it out.

The wind still hauling aft, [say abeam]: *Lay aft to the braces—weather main and lee cross-jack braces.* Hands by lee braces, after bowlines, main tack and sheet, studded sail tacks and sheets: *Clear away the after bowlines—brace in.* After yards being trimmed: *Head braces, clear away head bowlines—brace in. Trim the head yards by the main, sir* [to officer of forecastle]. Head yards being trimmed: *Get the topmast studding sail ready for setting.* The forecastlemen get the sail out ready for setting, the boom ready for going out, bend on the halliards, &c.; the foretopmen hook the burton, and overhaul down the halliards; the quarter gunners get the tack and boom brace aft; the mate of the forecastle mans the out-jigger, halliards and tack. When the sail is reported ready, command: *Haul taut—rig out and hoist away.* When the sail is above the fore brace, the squilgee is hauled out, tack gotten out, and sail hoisted taut up; the short sheet rove and trimmed down; the long sheet and downhaul sent down on deck; boom brace steadied; heel lashing passed, &c. The officer of the deck must not forget the *helm* when hauling out the tack and hoisting the sail.

The wind still hauling aft, (say on the quarter,) command: *Lay aft to the braces.* Brace in as before, observing to take in slack of tack, boom brace, and short sheet of topmast studding sail: *Man the weather main clew-garnet—spanker brails—haul taut—haul up—brail up.* The lee lifts must now be steadied, backstays set up, trusses and rolling tackles hauled taut, &c. &c. *Get the lower studding sail ready for setting.* The lower boom topping lift is hooked to guys, cut adrift; the outhaul is rove, and block for the short sheet put on (if not already on); the outer and inner halliards are overhauled down; the sail got out; outer halliards bent and inner ones hooked, and outhaul bent. Man well outer halliards and outhaul, lower boom topping lift, and forward guy; a few hands at the inner halliards; tend the squilgee, sheets, and after guy. *Haul taut, top up, rig out, and hoist away.* The boom is topped up, hauled forward, and trimmed with the fore yard; the sail run up by the outer halliards, squilgee hauled out, outhaul hauled close and sail hoisted taut up, inner halliards and sheet trimmed. Haul taut topmast studding sail boom topping lift, if not taut before. The men from the lower boom topping lift and forward guy can assist in setting the sail, if necessary.

Wind directly astern: *Lay aft to the braces—weather main and lee cross-jack braces.* Hands by the braces, &c. &c., as before. *Clear away after bowlines, square the after yards; head braces, clear away head bowlines, square away.* The after guy and outhaul must be manned, and forward guy tended, in addition to what has already been mentioned in bracing in. The head yards being square: *Man lee main clewgarnet and buntlines, head downhauls, haul taut—up mainsail—clear away the halliards—haul down.* The yards must now be squared by the lifts and braces, trusses, &c. &c., hauled taut. Get spanker boom amidships, backstays set up, &c.

Get all the port studding sails ready for setting.

Everything being ready: *Haul taut, rig out, and sway to hand.* The lower boom is topped up, hauled forward and trimmed, studding sail booms rigged out, and topmast and topgallant studding sails swayed to the yards, the outer stops cut, sails launched over the braces, and slack of tacks taken down. Men from lower boom topping lift, forward guy and out-jiggers, man lower studding sail halliards, &c.

Hoist away. The sails are hoisted together, properly set, and everything hauled taut.

QUESTION. What is the use of a burton on the topsail yard?

Q. Why steady the top-gallant bowline out before setting topgallant studding sail?

Q. What is a studding sail bend, and why is it used in preference to another?

Q. Upon taking the deck, what would you "look to" in order to see that the sails were properly set, rigging taut, &c., *by the wind?*

Q. Do., ship with all starboard studding sails set?

Q. Do., studding sails set both sides?

Q. In hauling out topmast studding sail afresh, how proceed, strong or fresh breeze? Wind abeam.

Q. Will the ship steer better when the wind is aft, or worse?

Q. Why have you hauled down the jibs?

Q. How is the topmast studding sail boom rigged in and out? and how is the heel lashing passed?

WIND HAULS FORWARD.

11. WIND DRAWS ON PORT QUARTER—SHIP UNDER SAIL, AS MADE IN THE PRECEDING ARTICLE.

The officer of the deck commands: *Stand by to dip the starboard topmast and top-gallant studding sails;* the tacks and

halliards being tended, and men on the yards. *Lower away.*
The tacks are eased off, to allow the men to get hold of the
outer leaches, and the yards being dipped forward: *Hoist away:*
then trim everything as before. Wind still hauling forward:
Stand by to take in the starboard studding sails. Man lower
studding sail clewline, after guy, a few hands on inner halliards
and sheet; topmast studding sail downhaul and long sheet, boom
jiggers, top-gallant studding sail tripping lines and sheets.
Hands by halliards, tacks, outhaul, forward guy, heel lashings,
short sheet in top, lower boom topping lift and boom brace:
Haul taut—let go the outhaul clew up. The lower studding
sail is clewed up, and just before the clew reaches the yard:
Lower away—haul down. All halliards are started together,
and just before the topmast studding sail yard is down to the
boom end: *Rig in.* The booms are rigged in, and lower boom
got alongside.

The topmen make up top-gallant studding sails aloft, secure
the booms, take the burton off, hitch topmast studding sail halliards to the clew of the sail, take the jigger off starboard top-
gallant lifts; fore yardmen secure studding sail boom: the lower
and topmast studding sails are made up and stowed away, and
the gear triced up.

Wind still hauling forward [say on quarter]: *Starboard head
braces.* The lee bowlines are overhauled, starboard fore sheet,
port fore tack, forward guy manned. Hands by weather head
braces, studding sail tacks and sheets, boom brace, after guy
and outhaul, weather trusses and lee lifts: *Brace up.* The
head yards trimmed: *Starboard main port cross-jack braces.*
Braces, &c., tended as before: *Brace up.* The yards trimmed,
the lower boom is trimmed by the fore yard, and all properly
set forward by the mate of the forecastle: *Man the head halliards, main sheet and spanker outhauls; haul taut: clear
away the downhauls, hoist away; let go the rigging, haul aft,
clear away the brails, haul out.* Trim the sails just set.

Wind *freshens*: it becomes necessary to take in the studding
sail: *Man the lower studding sail clewline and after guy.* Rigging being manned and tended, the officer of the deck will put
the helm up, and bring the wind a little on the starboard quarter, [*if he is fearful of carrying away the boom, and he has the
Captain's permission to run the ship off her course*]: *Haul
taut, clear away the outhaul, clew up; lower away, haul down,
rig in.* Then bring the ship on her course again.

If it is not possible to run the ship off, (sailing in squadron,
for instance,) the officer of the deck will get a *good pull* of the
after guy before starting anything, then *ease away* the outhaul

steadily and walk the clewline up, and lower the outer halliards with the same precautions. The sail is made up and gear triced up.

Wind hauls forward (say abeam). The officer of the deck will caution the man at the helm to "keep her full:" *See head braces* all manned and tended as before; *brace up*—easing the weather braces carefully. *After braces main tack, brace up and haul aboard main tack* as before, and see everything properly set, sheets trimmed aft, tacks gotten down, lee backstays borne abaft, lee lifts and rolling tackle (if hooked,) well overhauled, royal shrouds well set up, and halliards shifted to windward.

Wind freshens: *Stand by to take in royals, flying-jib and top-gallant studding sails,* the royal clewlines and weather braces being manned, lee braces and halliards tended, flying jib downhaul manned and hand by the halliards, topmen ready to take in studding sails, as before explained. *Haul taut—in royals, down flying jib—lower away, haul down, rig in.*

The yards are pointed to the wind, halliards and sheets let go together: *Furl the royals—stow the flying-jib.* The topmen make up the studding sail, &c., &c., as before explained.

The topmast studding sail boom may now be supported by using the lower studding sail halliards as a martingale.

Wind hauls forward: *Man the topmast studding sail downhaul.* Man and tend the gear, as before explained. Lower steadily and ease off the tack in the same manner. In this, as in other cases of taking in sail, the officer of the deck must be very attentive to the helm. A few spokes either way assists materially in facilitating the operation. The studding sail stowed away and gear triced up, the officer of the deck will brace the yards sharp up, beginning forward, as before. When getting the tacks down, *luff her well up.* The upper yards will be kept in, and all rigging set well taut.

QUESTION. What would you be careful about when bracing a yard, if there should be a man on it?

Q. Why get a pull of the after guy *before* starting anything, in taking in lower studding sail (fresh breeze)?

Q. Suppose the lower boom *flies under the bows?*

Q. How use the lower studding sail halliards to support the topmast studding sail boom?

Q. Make up lower, topmast and top-gallant studding sail for setting.

Q. How is the gear *triced up?*

Q. Blowing fresh, under top-gallant sails, you wish to get a *good pull of your* top-gallant breast backstays; what do?

Q. Blowing fresh, under top-gallant sails, you wish to *set up* your after top-gallant backstays; what do?

Q. *How* would you set them up?

Q. Under royals and flying-jib, wind freshens, the flying jib-boom *buckles;* you wish to set up the guys afresh. What do? and how set them up?

12. BY THE WIND UNDER TOP-GALLANT SAILS, COURSES, JIB AND SPANKER; SINGLE REEF THE TOPSAILS.

Man the top-gallant clewlines and weather braces ; haul taut, in top-gallant sails. The bowlines, sheets and halliards are let go, sails clewed up, yards pointed to the wind, top-gallant buntlines hauled up; but the sails not furled.

Man the topsail clewlines and weather braces. All being ready: *Haul taut—clear away the bowlines, round in the weather braces—settle away the topsail halliards—clew down.* The man at the wheel is directed to luff, in order to assist in bracing in; the topsail yards are braced in until they are nearly square, and the halliards hauled taut and belayed as soon as the yards are down—as is also the lee topsail brace.

Haul out the reef tackles—haul up the buntlines; and the reef tackles being out, and buntlines up: *Aloft topmen—stand by to take one reef in the topsail—man the boom tricing lines—trice up—lay out and reef.* The men, being on the yard, light the sail over to windward, in order that the weather earing may be passed; when the man passing it has taken several turns, he passes the word "haul out to leeward," and the lee earing being sufficiently out, the word is given by the man at it, to "tie away." The sail is gathered well up on the yard, and reef points tied with a square knot or half bow, observing to tie clear of the top-gallant sheets. In passing an earing, the earing is first taken out, over the cleet, down abaft the yard, through the cringle, up over the cleet again, down abaft, and the bight passed through the cringle, leaving the end abaft the sail. Pass the bight up before and over the yard, rousing the reef well up, haul back on the end until the bight lies close down on the yard, pass the end through the bight from abaft, haul well back and hitch it. In passing the earing for the 3rd and 4th reefs, take as many inner turns as the cringle will admit of, and pass the turns on the end—*not* on the bight. The topsails are to be kept *spilled* while reefing by the helmsman.

The sails being reefed: *Stand by the booms; lay in—down booms—lay down from aloft.* The heels of the booms are secured as soon as down. The topsail halliards are led along while the men are reefing. *Man the topsail halliards, let go and overhaul the rigging. tend the braces, haul taut, hoist away.* The yards are eased forward by the weather braces, rigging overhauled aloft, &c., and ship luffed up while hoisting When up: *Man the top-gallant sheets and halliards, sheet home and hoist away.* Trim the sails, haul taut everything. &c.. &c.

Note.—Before rounding in the weather braces, it is a good plan to settle a little of the halliards, particularly when reefing with the watch. With all hands on deck, the topmen may be sent aloft while chewing down; but in blowing weather, *always* lay the yards, and prepare the sail for reefing, *before* allowing a man on the yard.

Never brace or lower a yard with the men on it.

QUESTION. How do you pass the earing for the 4th reef?
Q. Part the reef tackle in hauling it out; what do?
Q. How trim the yards after hoisting?
Q. What precaution adopted when hoisting after reefing?
Q. Can the topsails be reefed without clewing up the top-gallant sails?
Q. How would you lay the fore topsail yard for reefing, as mate of the forecastle?
Q. How do you judge of a sail's being up?
Q. Before the wind, single reef the topsails,
Q. Wind on quarter, single reef the topsails.

13. TO REEF TOPSAILS IN STAYS.

Call "all hands 'bout ship and reef topsails;" station one watch of topmen for going aloft—hands by the topsail halliards: *Ready about—ready, ready—helms-a-lee. aloft topmen, rise tacks and sheets, overhaul lifts and trusses, bear abaft breast backstays, haul taut, mainsail haul, lower away the topsails*—(fore topsail clewlines must be well manned.) Lay the topsail yards, *haul out the reef tackles, haul up the buntlines, trice up, lay out and reef—head braces and topsail halliards: lay in—down booms—lay down from aloft; haul taut—let go and haul—hoist away the topsails.* Brace up and trim sharp as before.

Note—If there should be much wind, the fore topsail could not be *properly* reefed by following the above method; and in this case it would be better to clew down the main and mizen topsails as before, and not clew down the fore topsail until the order "Let go and haul," then "Lay out and reef," after which, hoist it—the main and mizen being hoisted as soon as reefed.

QUESTION.—What is the objection, if any, to clewing down

when the order is given, "Rise tacks and sheets," and swinging the main yard while the men are on the topsail yard?

Q. What is the objection to *letting go* the topsail halliards when the order is given to "ease down the helm," as in Murphy, page 18.

14. TO TAKE IN TOP-GALLANT SAILS, BLOWING FRESH.

Man the top-gallant clewlines and weather braces. When ready: *Haul taut—clear away the bowline, lee sheet and halliards—clew down;* and when the yard is down, and the clewline up: *Clear away the weather sheet—clew up.* The yard is pointed to the wind, lee brace steadied, top-gallant buntline hauled up: *Furl the top-gallant sails.*

QUESTION. Take in top-gallant sails before the wind.

Q. Why do you let go the lee sheet first?

Q. By the wind, under top-gallant sails, weather top-gallant sheet parts.

15. TO TAKE IN THE SPANKER, BLOWING FRESH.

*Man the spanker brails and head downhaul—ease away the outhauls—brail up—*lee brails best.

If the head of the sail does not brail in, but is seized to the gaff, it will be well to round in the lee cross jack brace, to prevent the sail flying over the lee yard arm.

To reef a spanker, haul the boom amidships, haul taut lee topping lift, lower peak and throat halliards, ease off the outhaul, pass the outer and inner earings, (if used,) observing *not* to pass the former round *the boom*, gather the sail up, and knot the points on the foot rope—hoist up taut, &c., &c.

16. TO TAKE IN THE JIB, AND SET FORE TOPMAST STAYSAIL.

Man the jib downhaul, fore topmast staysail halliards—haul taut—clear away the downhaul—hoist away—clear away the halliards—haul down. The jib sheet should be eased off as the sail comes down. In setting the staysail, first haul aft the sheet, and ease it off as the sail goes up.

To take in and *stow* a jib when *blowing hard*, it is always better *to run the ship off*, if possible.

QUESTION. Jib downhaul parts; what do?

Q. Jib sheet parts—by the wind.

Q. Jib splits—by the wind.

17. The breeze freshens; take the second reef in the topsails.

Proceed as in taking in the first reef. Put jiggers on the topsail lifts, and haul them taut.

18. To reef the courses.

Man the fore and main clewgarnets and buntlines—haul taut—up courses; haul the clewgarnets about two-thirds up; *haul out the reef tackles—aloft lower yardmen.* See the lifts, trusses, braces and rolling tackles well taut. *Trice up—lay out and reef.* The reef earings are passed on the end, out over a hook on the yard arm, back through the cringle, &c., as with a topsail. The reef points are taken with a round turn round the jackstay, and half hitched to the standing part. The sail being reefed: *Lay in—down booms—lay down from aloft.*
Man the tacks and sheets, and set the sails.
If the yard is to be braced in to clear the sail of the stays, do so *before* the men lay out on the yard.
Question. Why haul the clewgarnets only two-thirds up?

19. To take the third reef in the topsails.

Proceed as before, observing not to brace the topsail or lower yards too sharp up. Now get the preventor braces and parrals (if fitted,) on. Get rolling ropes on the top-gallant yards, if still aloft, and hook the rolling tackles.

20. To haul up and furl the mainsail.

Man the main clewgarnets and buntlines. The weather clewgarnet, both buntlines and leechlines are manned. Before starting anything, haul taut the lee main lift—ease off a fathom or two of the main sheet; *haul taut—ease away the main tack and bowline—haul up to windward.* The lee buntline is hauled up as far as it will go, and leechlines hauled taut: *Ease away the sheet—haul up to leeward.* After the sail is snug up: *Aloft main yardmen—trice up—lay out and furl.*
It is usual to set the main topsail after hauling up the mainsail.
Question. Why do you haul taut lee main lift?
Q. Why ease off a little of the main sheet?
Q. How would you heave to in a gale?

Q. Under what sail?
Q. How and under what sail scud?
Q. By the wind under all sail; heave to.
Q. Before the wind under all sail; heave to.
Q. By the wind—a man falls overboard.
Q. Before the wind—a man falls overboard.

31. BY THE WIND UNDER DOUBLE REEFED TOPSAILS AND COURSES; TO TURN A REEF OUT OF THE TOPSAILS.

Wishing to turn a reef out, the officer of the deck commands: *Aloft and stand by to turn a reef out of the topsails—Man the weather topsail braces, buntlines and reef-tackles—Hands by the topsail halliards.* All being manned the helmsman is is directed to *Luff*, and the command given: *Brace in—settle a little of the halliards—haul up the buntlines—haul out the reef tackles.*

The yards are braced a little in; a fathom or so of the halliards settled; the buntlines hauled taut, and the reef-tackles out—*Lay out and turn out one reef.* The men lay out and cast off from the *bunt out;* the outer yardmen single the earings, (being careful not to slack them off until ordered,) and the halliards are led along. When the "points" are all cast off, the men at the earings notify the officer of the deck that they are ready for "easing away," who commands: *Man the topsail halliards—Tend the braces—Ease away—Lay in—Lay down from aloft—Let go and overhaul the gear;* and as soon as the men are in off the yard: *Hoist away.*

The sails are hoisted, yards trimmed, &c., &c.

QUESTION. Why are the yards braced in and sails lowered?
Q. Why cast off from the bunt out?
Q. Why are the reef-tackles hauled out?
Q. How do you judge of the sail being up?
Q. Blowing fresh—set the mainsail.
Q.   do.   set the topgallant sails.
Q.   do.   set jib.
Q.   do.   set spanker.

32. HEAD TO WIND AND TIDE, GET UNDER WEIGH AND STAND OUT ON A WIND.

Before getting under weigh, the top-gallant and royal yards are crossed, cat-fall overhauled, messenger passed, other anchor ready for letting go, capstan bars shipped and swiftered in, nippers gotten up, &c. Having called all hands "Up Anchor," command: *Man the bars;* and send word to the Master to "bring to." There should be a man in each top, leadsmen in the chains, men at wheel, Quartermaster at signals and conn, Boatswain on forecastle, &c., &c.

When reported ready, command: *Heave round,* and send word to the Master to let you know when in to a short scope—naming the scope from which you wish to make sail. The chain is unbitted as it comes in, stoppers taken off, and chain paid below, (unless very muddy.) The topmen stationed to pass or put on nippers, should work fast enough to allow the men at the capstan to heave round briskly without stopping. As soon as the chain is into the required scope, command: *Avast heaving—Pawl the Capstan*—and have the capstan bars unshipped on the spar deck. Direct the Boatswain to call all hands "make sail;" when men are up from below: *Aloft sail loosers—Trice up—Lay out and loose,* (from royals down, if the wind will permit,) *Man the sheet halliards.* When the sails are reported ready: *Haul taut—Let fall—Sheet home and hoist away—Lay in—Down booms—Down from aloft.* The sails should all be sheeted home and hoisted together, but if short-handed, the topsails first, then the topgallant sails and royals. The spanker is loosed and boom gotten on the proper quarter; the jibs loosed and halliards led along. The sails being hoisted well up, sheets home, &c., command, (supposing the ship to be lying by the starboard anchor and we have room enough to cast either way,): *Man the starboard fore and cross-jack—port main braces—brace abox—brace up.* The head yards are braced abox and the after yards up; and when done, the spar deck bars are shipped: *Man the bars—Heave around.* When the anchor is nearly up and down, direct the helmsman to give her a sheer with the starboard helm. When the ship is directly over her anchor, the officer of the forecastle notifies the officer of the deck that the anchor is "up and down;" then: *Man the jib and flying-jib halliards.* As soon as the anchor is off the ground, the officer of the forecastle says: "Anchor's aweigh," and the command is given: *Clear away the downhauls—hoist away.* The jibs are hoisted and weather sheets kept aft, and the helm shifted as soon as sternboard commences. The anchor is run up to the bows, catted and fished. If there is room, the head yards should be squared, spanker set, and head sheets let go while the anchor is being fished, (unless the wind should be very light.) The command is given: *Man the port head braces* just before the after yards fill, and as they fill: *Brace round.* The helm is righted as soon as she has fallen off sufficiently far.

The anchor having been fished and head yards braced up,

command: *Man the fore and main tacks and sheets;* and when manned: *Haul taut—Clear away the rigging—Haul aboard.* The courses having been set, braces, lifts, trusses, &c., attended to, clear up the decks and pipe down.

QUESTION. Station the crew for getting under weigh.
Q. Why is the other anchor gotten ready for letting go?
Q. Station the officers: say, in a frigate.
Q. You are Master of a ship, and are ordered to get ready for heaving up; what preparations would you make?
Q. How are the bars shipped and "swiftered in?" *Why* "swiftered in"?
Q. What officer attends to rigging the capstan?
Q. What officer attends to passing the messenger?
Q. What officer attends to the jig-back?
Q. Reeve the cat and fish falls.
Q. How is the messenger passed?
Q. What are the different kinds of nippers used, and how are they passed and put on?
Q. What is meant by "bringing to"?
Q. Lying in five fathoms water, from what scope would you make sail?
Q. What is "pawling the capstan"?
Q. What is a nix stopper.
Q. A nipper jambs; how clear it?
Q. Why do you cast *from* your anchor?
Q. How do you cat and fish an anchor?
Q. What is meant by "surging" the messenger?
Q. Bend and unbend chain cables.
Q. When is the anchor "a-peak;" "a-weigh;" "up and down;" "a-trip"?
Q. Standing in on starboard tack, under all sail anchor.
Q. Standing in before the wind; anchor.
Q. Get under weigh and stand out before the wind.

Part IV.

MASTER'S DUTIES.

HINTS FOR YOUNG MASTERS.

MASTER'S DUTIES.

Commissioning:—Upon reporting for duty to the commandant of the station at which the vessel is fitting out, the Master should copy from the "Allowance Book" a list of all articles belonging to his department. He should at once make himself acquainted with the master, boatswain and other officers of the yard, and note the various buildings in which masters' stores are stowed, and from which he will draw his own. He should find out from the naval constructor the supposed best sailing time of his vessel; the peculiarities of construction (if any); the rake of her masts, and quantity of water stowed; and, if the vessel has before made a cruise, he should procure the report of her captain made out in the form prescribed in the C. S. Navy Regulations. In a word, he should possess himself of all the information to be gained from officers acquainted with the properties of the vessel.

If the stowage has not been commenced, he will personally superintend it and note in his remark book the quantity of ballast, water, provisions, &c., taken in. When the tanks are filled, he will *see* that none are overlooked. While stowing, he should bear in mind the best sailing time of the vessel and try so to stow her as to produce the proposed difference of draft. After the hold and spirit-room are stowed, he will receive from the master of the yard a *plan*, which he will thereafter keep in his possession.

He should enter in his note book the number and weight of all anchors, kedges and grapnels; the size and length of the chain cables and how the *ends* are made fast; the size and number of hemp cables, hawsers, towlines, &c; the number and kind of stoppers, nippers, hook-ropes, chain-hooks, &c; and see that all of the above are properly fitted and stowed.

The messenger is fitted by the gunner; but the master should examine it and see that it is in working order and that "jig-backs" are provided.

The "clear-hawse" gear, mooring-swivel and spare bolts and spackles should be examined and stowed in a convenient place for getting out when wanted.

It is customary for the master to select the signal quarter-master from the number appointed by the executive officer. With his assistance he will receive and stow the following articles, most of which are generally placed in his immediate charge, viz:

Signal halliards, leads and lines, log reels and lines, 14 and 28-second glasses, ensigns, spare bunting and muslin, needles and thread, signals, flags of all nations, artificial horizon, chronometers, tunic pieces, barometers, thermometers, hydrometers, sextants, log-book, stationery, nautical books, instruments and charts, spy glasses, lanterns (signal and deck), compasses (boat, binnacle and azimuth), tell-tales, binnacles, wheel ropes, relieving tackles, &c., &c., &c.

The galley comes also in the master's department and should be looked after and the cooking utensils distributed among the different messes. So also the cabin, ward-room and steerage furniture.

The Book of Allowance will serve to call the master's attention to various other matters pertaining to his department. He should be able to answer inquiries as to all the stores in his charge; where everything is stowed; number and weight of; how fitted, &c., &c., &c.

The following is a copy of the master's duties taken from the "Regulations for the Navy of the Confederate States," approved April 29, 1862.

MASTER.

The master, or the officer appointed to perform his duties, will, if ordered to a vessel before her stowage is commenced, superintend, under the direction of the commanding officer of the yard or commanding the vessel as circumstances may require, the stowing of the ballast, water, provisions, and all other articles in the hold and spirit-room.

In stowing provisions he shall take care that the oldest be stowed so that they may be first issued; breaking out and restowing those already on board if necessary for these purposes, unless otherwise directed.

When the stowage of the hold shall be completed, an entry

must be made in the log-book specifying particularly the quantity and arrangement of the ballast, the number, size and disposition of the tanks and casks, and of the quantity and stowage of provisions and other stores.

Accurate plans must be made of the stowage of the hold, showing the disposition of all the articles, which must be inserted in the first page of the log-book; and if any material change should afterwards be made in the stowage, the change must be noted, and new plans inserted in the log-book.

If the stowage of the hold is made under the direction of the commandant of the yard, the commander of the vessel is to be furnished with the plans and descriptions.

If made at a navy yard, but under the direction of the commander of the vessel, he will furnish the commanding officer of the yard with them, that they may be inserted in the diary of the yard.

The master is to visit the hold daily and cable tiers and chain lockers very frequently, and see that they are kept in as good order as circumstances will admit.

He shall have charge of the keys of the hold and spirit-room, and shall only deliver them to a commission or warrant officer.

He is under the direction of the commanding or executive officer, to see that the cables are at all times properly secured and protected from injuries; that the tiers are kept clear, and that all necessary arrangements are made for anchoring, mooring, unmooring or getting under weigh with the greatest facility and dispatch.

He will, when directed, examine the chain cables, and particularly the shackles and shackle-pins, to see that they can be readily removed in case it should be necessary to ship the cables or shift parts from one cable to another.

He is in the same manner to see that the standing and running rigging, and the sails of the vessel, are at all times in good order, protected from injury and ready for service, and to report all such as may require alteration or repairs; and he will also attend in person to setting up the rigging.

He is to be particularly careful to present any waste or improper expenditure of fuel and water; and he is to report daily when at sea to the captain the quantity of each, except the fuel in charge of the engineer expended in the last twenty-four hours, and the quantity remaining on hand.

When the vessel shall be approaching any land or shoals, or entering any port or harbor, he shall be very attentive to the soundings; and he shall at all times inform the commander of any danger to which he may think the vessel exposed, whether under the charge of a pilot or not.

He shall examine the charts of all coasts which the vessel may visit, and note upon them any errors which he may discover and inform the commanding officer of the same, who shall transmit them to the Navy Department.

He shall frequently examine the compasses, time glasses, log and lead lines, and keep them in proper order for service.

He shall ascertain and report daily to the commanding officer the ship's place at meridian, and at any other time when the commanding officer may direct the variation of the compass, and the bearing and distance of the nearest head land, or any danger that may be near.

He is to have charge of and must account for all nautical books, instruments, charts, national flags and signals.

He shall have charge of keeping the ship's log-book, and shall see that all particulars are duly entered in it according to such forms as are or may be prescribed; and he shall immediately after such entries, send it to the watch officers that they may sign their names at the end of the remarks in their respective watches, when the circumstances are fresh in their memories; and he shall take it to the commanding officer for his inspection immediately after noon of each day.

There shall be entered on the log-slate and log-book, with minute exactness, the following particulars:

1. The name and rank or rating of all persons who may join or be discharged from the vessel; the names of all passengers, with time of coming on board, and leaving; the direction of the wind, state of the weather, courses steered and distances sailed; the time where any particular evolution, exercise or other service was performed; the signal numbers of all signals made; the time when, by what vessel, and to what vessel, they were made; nature and extent of public punishment inflicted, with the name and crime of the offence; the result of all observations made to find the ship's place, and all dangers discovered in navigation.

2. The groundings of the ship, and the loss of or serious injury to boats, spars, rigging and stores of any kind, with the circumstances under which they happened, and the extent of the injury received.

3. A particular account of all packages and stores received, with their marks, contents or quantities, and the apartment for which they were received.

4. A particular account of all stores condemned by survey,

5

or converted to any other purpose than that for which they were originally intended.

5. A particular account of all stores lent or otherwise sent or ent out of the vessel, and by what authority it was done.

6. All the marks and numbers of every cask or bale which on being opened, is found to contain less than is specified by invoice, or than it ought to contain, with the deficiency found.

7. Every alteration made in the allowance of provisions, and by whose order.

8. The employment of any hired vessel, her dimensions in tonnage, the name of the master or owner, the number of her crew, how or for what purpose employed, by whose order, and the reasons for her employment.

9. The draft of water of the vessel when light, as furnished from the navy yard, and always before going to sea, and upon arriving in port fore and aft; and the height of the forward part of the forward port-sills, after part of after port-sills, and of the mid-ship port-sills from the water; and the rake of the respective masts in every ten feet, with reference to the water-line at the time.

After the log has been signed by the officers of the watches, no alteration shall be made therein, except to correct some error or supply some omission, and then only with the approbation of the commanding officer, or the recollection of the officer who had charge of the watch in which the alteration or addition is proposed, who will sign the same if satisfied of its correctness.

The master will deliver to the commanding officer of the vessel, signed by himself, and after careful comparison, certified to be correct, a fair copy of the log-book, every six months, to be transmitted by the first safe opportunity to the Navy Department.

The original log-book shall be kept by the vessel until she is paid off, when it shall be placed in charge of the commanding officer of the yard, and by him transmitted to the Navy Department.

Besides the log-book, he is to keep a remark-book in which all the hydrographical information he can obtain is to be carefully inserted, as well as a description of the instruments he may employ in any of the observations hereafter mentioned.

He is to determine as accurately as he can the various particulars relating to navigation of every place which the vessel may visit entering the results in his remark-book under the following heads:

1. Latitude.
2. Longitude.

3. Variation of the compass.
4. Time of high water immediately following near and full moon.
5. Rise and fall of tides at spring and neaps.
6. Prevailing winds.
7. Periods of the year at which the wet and dry seasons prevail, if any.
8. Seasons at which hurricanes prevail.
9. The temperature of the chronometer room at the time observations are taken.

The particular spot at the place visited to which the latitude and longitude refer is to be carefully noted; also the number and nature of the observations, and the means by which they were made, whether the artificial or sea horison was used; and with reference to the longitude if obtained with chronometers by means of meridian distances from another place, he is to state the number employed, their general characters, the age of the rates used, or the interval since which they were last rated, with the longitude he has assumed of the place measured from.

He is not to loose any opportunity of obtaining lunar distances, both with the view of determining the longitude the ship may be in at sea, as well as serving as a saluting comparison with his chronometers either at sea or in harbor.

He is to observe the variations of the compass by amplitudes or azimuths at least once every year, whether at sea or in port, excepting only when refitting in harbor. The azimuth compass is to be always placed when practicable in the same precise situation amid ships, making the point where each of the tripod legs stands; and he is to take care that the direction of the ship's head at the time of observation shall be recorded, as well as the difference between the standard or azimuths, and the steering compasses, by which precaution alone can the real course of the ship be regulated. These variations are to be daily inserted in columns at the end of his remark-book along with the ship's place, and the direction of her head at the time of observation.

The local attraction is to be determined before the ship leaves the Confederate States, as well as after any material change of latitude, and is there to be tabulated by him for every point of the compass, so that the corrections on each course may be readily applied in working the ship's reckoning.

In all places he is to ascertain the direction and velocity of the currents, the set and strength of the tides, with the limits of their rise and fall, and the time of high water of the tide which immediately follows the periods of the new and full moons. He is to describe, as particularly as he can, the appearances of foreign coasts, pointing out the remarkable objects by which they may be distinguished, so as to render a stranger certain of recognizing his land fall.

He is to apply to the captain, when the service will admit of it, for boats to sound and survey any shoals or harbors which have not been correctly laid down in the charts, and the results are to be projected on a large and intelligible scale.

In his remark-book he is carefully to note all inaccuracies in any of the charts supplied to the ship.

He is frequently to present this remark-book to the captain for examination; and on the first of January in every year he is to deliver to him a correct copy of it; accompanied by all the charts, plans and views of the coast and head lands which he has made during the past year; all which the captain will transmit by the first safe opportunity to his commander-in-chief, to be forwarded to the Department.

He shall not be required to keep watches except in cases of necessity, and then only by order of the commander of the vessel.

Every vessel before sailing shall be furnished with a skeleton chart, embracing her probable cruising ground, on which shall be laid down her track and daily run during the whole time of her absence, which chart shall be transmitted to the Navy Department at the end of the cruise.

Should the master be removed or suspended, he shall sign the log-book and deliver it to his successor, taking his receipt for the same, and for all other articles under his charge, and shall deliver to his commander a fair copy of the remark-book, made up to the day of his removal or suspension.

MASTER'S DUTIES—IN PORT.

The master should examine the state of the rigging, and report to the executive officer every morning before breakfast. He should wind up and set the deck time-piece at a regular hour—say at 7.45 A. M. Various methods are adopted by masters for the purpose of reminding them of this important duty. [A good plan is to keep your tooth-brush in the chronometer box.]

He should write up the log in the form prescribed by the Ordnance Office, and send it in daily; visit the holds; keep the ship filled up with wood and water; keep the expenditures of each; examine the yeoman's account of other expenditures in his department; see that the keys of the holds are put in his room at sunset; look to the anchors and chains; take observations for rating the chronometers; take the ship's draft every four or five days, and particularly just before leaving port, or after entering; attend to any work going on in his department—such as "clearing hawse," receiving stores, transporting anchors, weighing an anchor with the launch, &c., &c., and at 8 P. M. report to the executive officer the state of the anchors and chains.

His leisure time should be employed in arranging the different articles in his department, and attending to various matters pertaining to his duties, some of which are specified below:

1. *Rating Chronometers.*

Books on navigation generally recommend rating by "Equal Altitudes," but masters seldom adopt that method. The method by single altitudes (observing that A. M. should not be combined with P. M. observations,) is the most convenient and most accurate—unless the observer has had considerable experience in "Equal Altitude" observations.

Observations should be taken at intervals of seven or ten days, and a set taken the day before going to sea.

After receiving the chronometers, the masters will generally find that the rates are different from those sent from the store or ordnance office. If there should be a very great change, the fact should be reported. They should be carefully stowed, and compared each morning.

Having established the "Errors" and "Rates" enter them in your book, and before going to sea compare the errors for some days in advance—in the following form: (See page 70.)

Date.	Chro. 2971, or A	Chro. 1853, or B	Chro. 3411, or C
Oct. 19, 1863.	Fast 3m. 05s. Daily loss 3s.3.	Fast 17m. 30s. 3. Daily gain 7s. 1.	Slow 30m. 30s. 5 Daily loss, 17s. 5
Oct. 19	h m s — 0. 03. 05. 0 — 3. 3	h m s — 0. 17. 30. 3 + 7. 1	h m s + 0. 30. 30. 5 + 17. 5
20	3. 1. 7 3. 3	17. 37. 4 7. 1	30. 48. 0 17. 5
21	2. 58. 4 3. 3	17. 44. 5 7. 1	31. 05. 5 17. 5
22	2. 55. 1 3. 3	17. 51. 6 7. 1	31. 23. 0 17. 5
23	2. 51. 8 3. 3	17. 58. 7 7. 1	31. 40. 5 17. 5
24	2. 48. 5 3. 3	18. 05. 8 7. 1	31. 58. 0 17. 5
25	2. 45. 2 3. 3	18. 12. 9 7. 1	32. 15. 5 17. 5
26	2. 41. 9 3. 3	18. 20. 0 7. 1	32 33. 0 17. 5
27	2. 38. 6 3. 3	18. 27. 1 7. 1	32. 50. 5 17. 5
28	2. 35. 3 3. 3	18. 34. 2 7. 1	33. 08. 0 17. 5
29	2. 32. 0 3. 3	18. 41. 3 7. 1	33. 25. 5 17. 5
30	2. 28. 7	18. 48. 4	33. 43. 0

The algebraic sign indicates how the "Error" is to be applied to the "Face of the Chro." Example:

COMPARISON OF CHRONOMETERS. *Oct'r 27th, 1863.*

Chro. 2971, or A.	Chro. 1853, or B.	Chro. 3411, or C.
h m s	h m s	h m s
Face of	Face of	Face of
Chro. 13. 53. 49. 0	Chro. 14. 09. 39. 0	Chro. 13. 18. 19. 0
Error — 2. 38. 6	Error — 18. 27. 1	Error + 32. 50. 5
Gr time 13. 51. 10. 4	Gr time 13. 51. 11. 9	Gr time 13. 51. 09. 5

The mean of the three chronometers is assumed for the mean Greenwich time, unless there is reason to believe that one of the three is in error.

Instead of designating the Chronometers by their numbers, use the letters A, B, C, keeping a note of the numbers and the names of the makers.

2. *Time of Sunset:*

For the convenience of the officer of the deck, the Master should compute the mean time of sunset for a number of days in advance, tabulate it, and hang it at the cabin door in charge of the orderly. The time of daylight can be found, if required, by computing the hour at which the sun crossed the crepusculum.

3. *Ensigns, Signals, &c.:*

The Master should have made up at least three national ensigns for the ship, and one for each boat, together with the necessary flags or pendants. If in a flag ship, make up the distinguishing pendant of each vessel in the squadron.

Examine the numbers and repeaters, and see them properly fitted with toggles and distance-lines; also, have everything ready for making night signals.

4. *Leads and Lines:*

Note the different kinds of deep-sea leads, mark the lines and stow them away. Measure and mark the hand-lead lines; fit a couple of sling bands for the leadsmen, and have two of them always at hand; as a "drift" lead and line.

5. *Log Reels and Lines.*

Examine the reels and mark the lines as directed in Bowditch's Navigator. Have two reels put in place on deck before going to sea.

Test the accuracy of the 14th and 28th second glasses.

6. *Sextants and other Nautical Instruments.*

Examine the condition of the sextants, adjust them, and keep the one intended for every day use at hand. Examine the state of the barometer, thermometers, hydrometers and boxes of instruments. Before sailing, place a chart tell-tale, box of instruments, sailing directions, and spy-glass, in the cabin.

7. *Charts and Sailing Directions.*

The charts should be examined, to see that the proper ones have been sent, and then stowed away—keeping the ones first to be used on top. Compare those in use with each other, and with your table of latitudes and longitudes; note the errors and differences. Keep the harbor charts separate from the others.

Before sailing, the Master should consult the "Sailing Directions," so as to be able to advise the Commander as to the proper route to be pursued—he should be able to answer any questions in relation to the prevailing winds, currents, &c., along the route.

Good navigation consists not merely in finding the ship's daily position; it requires a knowledge of the winds and currents of the ocean; the faculty of predicting the changes of weather, &c., &c.

The Master, then, should diligently *study* the "Sailing Directions," the law of storms, the wind and current charts, &c., &c., and should be a careful observer of the weather, and of all the phenomena attending.

8. *Steering Gear.*

Nothing is of more importance than that the steering gear should be in good order. The master should attend personally to reeving the wheel-ropes, fitting spare ones and placing the relieving tackles handy. Stow the spare tiller where it can be quickly gotten at.

Examine state of wheel-ropes frequently; oil them, (if of hide,) and before getting underweigh heave the wheel over two or three times.

9. *Marking Chains.*

In the U. S. Navy the chains were marked at the foundry, for every fathom, in raised figures or letters. As the chains supplied our vessels are not, however, usually marked at all, the Master will have it to do after receiving them aboard.

The best plan, I think, is to mark them as follows, viz:

At the first, or 15th fathom shackle, put a mark with wire or spun-yarn on the *first link* forward of the shackle; at the second, or 30th fathom shackle, put the mark on the *second link;* at the third, or 45th fathom shackle, on the third; and so on. Put on as many turns of the wire or spun yarn as you think proper, and as long as *one lasts* you will be able to tell the number of the shackle *by counting the links.*

Another plan (and which should be combined with the above) is to mark the heads of the bolts of the shackles with a cold chisel—marking the first bolt I, the second II, and so on.

Chains should be examined once in six months. The starboard watch rousing up the starboard chains, the port watch the port ones. By providing long whips, and working one watch against the other, the work is soon done.

In examining the chains, see that the shackles are put in with the *bolts aft;* that the bolts are not rusted in; that the swivels will turn; (pour spirits of turpentine in to cause them to do so;) that no stay bolts are out, &c., and beat the rust off.

Examine the state of the end fastenings, clean out the lockers and stow them below again.

The spare shackles, mooring swivel, nippers, and everything relating to the ground-tackling, should be examined at the same time.

10. *Binnacles and Compasses.*

The Master should pay particular attention to the *placing of the binnacles;* the manner of lighting them; *their distance apart:* no iron in their vicinity; no "stow-holes" in the lower part, &c., &c. He should examine and compare all the compasses, fix the position of the "standard;" see that the "cards" travel freely; that they are properly balanced; that the sockets and spindles are in good order, and that the "cards" intended for the Azimuth Compass are marked A, B, C, &c.

The needles, when not suspended, should be put away in pairs, parallel, and with the North Pole of one against the South Pole of the other, and separated by a piece of cork or soft wood.

The following copy of a memorandum, issued by order of the Board of Admiralty, (English,) respecting placing compasses on board ship, removal of iron from their vicinity, &c., &c., will furnish all the information necessary:

MEMORANDUM.

Admiralty, Nov. 20, 1845.

With reference to the several orders which, from time to time, have been issued respecting the removal of iron from the vicinity of the compasses, placing the binnacle and standing compasses on board her Majesty's ships, &c.; and with the view of comprising these orders in one circular for the guidance of the officers concerned, my Lord's Commissioners of the Admiralty are pleased to direct—

"That no iron of any kind shall be placed, nor be suffered to remain, within the distance of seven feet of the binnacle or standard compasses, when it is practicable, according to the size and construction of the vessel, to remove it; and that mixed metal or copper be substituted for iron in the bolts, keys and dowels, in the scarphs of beams, coamings and head-ledges, and also the hoops of the gaffs and booms, and belaying-pins, which come within the distance of seven feet of the said compasses.

"The spindles and knees of the steering-wheels, which come within the distance of some seven feet of the compasses, are also to be of mixed metal.

"Iron tillers, which work forward from the rudder-head, are not to range within seven feet of the compasses; and in vessels which have iron tillers working abaft the rudder-head, the binnacles are to be placed as far forward from the wheel as may be convenient for the helmsman to steer by.

"The boat's iron davits are to be placed as far as may be practicable and convenient from the compasses.

"All vertical iron-stanchions, such as those for the support of the deck, or for the awnings, &c., and likewise the armstands, are to be kept beyond the distance of fourteen feet from the compasses in use, so far as the size of the vessel will admit.

"All steam vessels are to be fitted with hollow pillars for the support of their standard compasses, except in such cases as the Superintendent of the Compass Department shall point out, in which instances a solid wood pillar or mixed metal stanchions, for the support of a copper binnacle-head, is to be prepared, and those pillars or supports are to be so placed that the said binnacle-head will be in the midship line, and in such a position, forward or aft, as the Superintendent, upon consultation with the master-shipwright, shall think most advisable, according to the construction of the vessel and nature of her armament.

"In ships of the line and frigates, it having been found more convenient to place the standard compass in a copper binnacle, supported by mixed metal stanchions or a solid wood pillar, these are to be prepared according to the application of the Superintendent of the Compass Department.

"In brigs or other vessels, when the main-boom may prevent a standard or azimuth compass from being constantly kept at the proper elevation for observations, a solid pillar, made so as to unship, or a sliding tube, constructed so as to be capable of being lowered upon a short pillar, is to be prepared, whichever plan may be considered most suitable to the vessel, according to her equipment and armament.

"The binnacles for the steering compasses are to be constructed upon a given plan, with tops made to take off; and, in order to prevent improper materials from being deposited therein, they are not to be fitted with doors.

"As the vicinity of the compass, when the binnacles are too close together, has been found materially to affect their accuracy in all ships where there are two binnacles, they are to be separated as much as the diameter of the wheel will permit, and so as the helmsman may see the compass conveniently; but in no case are they to be allowed to be nearer than four feet six inches.

"For the better preservation of the compasses in every ship, a closet is to be constructed in a dry place, sufficiently large for the reception of the ship's establishment of compasses, and it is to be appropriated to that purpose exclusively, the key being kept by the Master; and in order that the space-compass cards may never be kept with poles of the same nearest to each other, cases, which prevent the possibility of their being packed improperly, (specimens of which have been sent to each yard,) are to be prepared.

"These regulations are to be alike applicable to ships ordered to be built, and to those directed to be prepared for commission, and the previous orders on this subject are to be considered cancelled.

"By command of their Lordships,

"H. CORRY."

It has been said that the Master should examine his compasses and compare them. The examination consists in:

1st. To determine the index error of the instrument. This correction is the same for all bearings, and may be found for each compass and compass card, by bearings of a number of objects in different directions, whose true magnetic bearing has been determined by more delicate instruments. Once carefully found, it may be marked as a *constant* correction.

2d. To correct for eccentricity, or for the pivot not being in the centre of the graduated circle. The maximum error may be found by measuring (with the Azimuth compass,) horizontal angles of about 90°, which have been measured by a more reliable instrument.

The Admiralty compass (a description of which is given below,) is furnished with the means of testing the eccentricity and the precision of graduation, in the graduated circle and its opposite reachings.

3d. To attend to the balancing of the compass card. The best compasses are furnished with small moveable counterpoises for this adjustment. Sealing-wax dropped on that part of the card which requires depression, is sometimes used.

As the North end of the needle dips, or is depressed in North magnetic latitude, and the South end in South magnetic latitude, re-adjustment is generally necessary after a considerable change of latitude.

4th. That the sight vane or vanes, and their axis of rotation, should be parallel, also perpendicular to the graduated circle, if there be one, on the compass box.

Observations on a plumb line, or other well defined vertical line made on the land, furnish a test of these adjustments.

5th. That the mirror should be perpendicular to the plane passing through the eye-vane and the thread of the sight-vane. This may be tested by observations on a well defined vertical line on shore.

The following brief description of the Admiralty compass will sufficiently denote the principles on which it is constructed:

The magnetic needles employed are compound bars, or lamina, of that kind of steel which has been ascertained by numerous experiments to be capable of receiving the greatest magnetic power, and the compass bowl is of copper, which is found to calm the vibrations of the needle to a considerable extent.

The interesting point of the axis of the gimbals is made to coincide with the point of suspension of the card, and also with the centre of the azimuth circle, and the impressions of the cards being taken off after the paper has been cemented to the mica, distortions by shrinking are prevented, and a more perfect centering is attained.

The points of the pivots are made of a material which is harder than steel, and which does not corrode by exposure to the atmosphere, and the ruby caps are worked to a form to suit the points.

Spare points of electrical steel are likewise supplied. These are gilded by the electrical process.

The cards and needles are adjusted to the magnetic meridian, in a place free from the local influence of iron.

The following instructions are issued with each compass:

"This instrument is so constructed as to answer the purpose of a steering compass and an azimuth compass, and it being in charge of the Captain or commanding officer, it is expected to be used with the care due to the nature of its construction, which has been briefly explained.

"I.—*When used as a Steering Compass.*

"Be very careful to preserve the *pivot-point* from injury when screwing the pivot into the bowl, and place the card gently upon it, and never move the compass without first having lifted the card (by means of the side screw,) against the centre-pin. This should be done also before any guns are fired.

"The pivots, caps, and margins of the cards should be examined occasionally to see that their free working is not impeded by dust or fibres from the paper; and, as each compass is furnished with two cards and six pivots, whenever the card works sluggishly, or injury by accident or long wear be suspected, the spare card or (as the case may be) a new cap or pivot should be put on. The central cap-screw, or nut on the face of the card, must be taken off before the ruby cap is attempted to be unscrewed.

"When the card A is not sufficiently steady, the heavy card J, with the particular pivot appropriated to it, is to be used.

"When the bowl does not work freely on its gimbals, the axis and their bushes should be examined and slightly rubbed with plumbago.

"The bottom of the box is made to take out, so that the compass, when placed in the binnacle, or on the standard pillar, may be lighted from below, if necessary.

"The cover of the bowl is fastened by bayonet notches, and is to be removed before the azimuth circle (which has its own glass cover) is put on.

"The card should be adjusted for dip by the balancing slides when necessary.

"II—*As an Azimuth Compass.*

"Any one of the compasses may be immediately converted to this purpose by lifting it upon its stand, removing the glass cover, and fixing the azimuth circle on its upper margin.

"In observing amplitudes and azimuths at sea, the bearings are read from the card, without reference to the external graduated circle.

"This instrument may also be used for surveying purposes. By adjusting the zero of the graduated circle to any given object, and clamping the instrument on its stand, with the screw prepared for that purpose, the angles of objects round the horizon may then be observed and read off to the nearest minute.

"Again—when accurate magnetic bearings on land are required, the zero of the circle may be adjusted to the magnetic North or South, shown by the card, and then clamped, thus any number of magnetic bearings round the circle may be obtained."

The Admiralty compass was furnished all vessels in the U. S. Navy, but it is probable that the Master will rarely see one in our service. Makers, however, generally send "directions" with their compasses, so that no difficulty will be met with in using them.

The following are the names of some of the best compasses (English) lately introduced: Walker's, West's, Dents', Stebbings' and Preston's liquid compass. Most boat-compasses are "liquid."

Before proceeding to describe the manner of finding the *deviation of the compass*, the following "hints" are introduced for the benefit of the Master, or other person, in charge of that important instrument.

Electricity will disturb the needle. If the glass cover be rubbed with dry silk, a delicate compass may be rendered for the time useless.

A strong electric current may weaken the magnetism of a needle, or even reverse its poles. Lightning may, *and has*, produced such a change.

When near volcanic islands the needle will be affected.

The *deviation* will be much more considerable in an iron vessel than in a wooden one, and should be very carefully observed.

The points of "no deviation" are not *necessarily* at or near the North or South points; some iron vessels have shown them to be near the *East and West points*. A piece of iron or tin in the binnacle will disturb the needle, so also will muskets stowed on the decks below.

Any change in the iron, such as moving guns, *swinging in* quarter-boats' *iron* davits, raising and lowering telescopic funnel, &c., will affect the compass.

The compasses being nearer each other than 4½ feet, will affect the needles.

If the ship (particularly if an iron one) is *heeled*, the compasses will be affected, therefore the "deviation" should be found with the ship in such positions.

In approaching the magnetic Equator, the "deviation" will *generally* decrease. After crossing the Equator, *West* deviation will become *East*, and *East* deviation *West*.

The "deviation" can be found at sea by placing the ship's

head on a particular course and observing an azimuth; the variation found compared with the variation marked on the chart, will show the "deviation" for that *particular course;* * in this

> * *Note.*—Remembering that the *variation found* is composed of the variation proper, ∓ *the deviation.*
> If the ship's head is placed on the point of "no deviation," (as previously found by swinging the ship) the variation found should agree with that marked on the chart, (always supposing the chart to give the correct variation.)

way the "deviation table" can be tested.

Standard compasses should be placed *at as great an elevation as possible.*

TO FIND THE DEVIATION OF THE COMPASS.

> NOTE. The student who may desire to pursue this subject farther, is referred to the following authorities:
> "Memoire sur les déviations de la boussole," par M. Poisson: "Account of Experiments on Iron-built ships;" by G. B. Airy, Esq.; "Practical Illustrations of the necessity for ascertaining the Deviations of the Compass; by Capt. Edward Johnson, R. N.; "Walker on the Magnetism of Ships;" and a number of Pamphlets edited by Mr. Archibald Smith, Major General Sabine, J. R. Napier, Esq., and others; published by order of the British Admiralty.
> Most of these works have been largely quoted from in preparing the article on "finding the Deviation."

The "Deviation" of the compass is the error caused by the influence of the ships iron upon the magnetic needle, and must not be confounded with the "variation. The extensive use of iron in ship-building—particularly in the Iron-clads—renders it absolutely necessary that the Deviation should be found and tabulated.

The following are some of the prominent sources of error in a ship's course, as relates to the compass, independently of those which may arise from tides, currents, or bad steerage.

I. The imperfections of the compasses themselves, the weakness of the magnetism of their needles, the distention of the compass cards, the occasional oblique direction of the magnetic axis in such as have flat bars, the imperfection of their pivots and caps, inefficient suspension, and balancing, and the want of concentricity in the general construction of the instrument.

II. Rough usage and inattention to the occasional examination of the pivots, caps, needles, and gimbals, the improper mode of keeping the cards, and also the erroneous supposition that correct bearings may be obtained from any part of a ship without having ascertained the *deviation* of the compass in the particular place from whence such bearings have been observed.

III. The errors caused by the reciprocal action of compasses upon each other, when (as is generally the case) the binnacles are placed too closely together.

IV. The errors produced when portions of iron work, or moveable pieces of iron, are improperly placed near the compass.

V. DEVIATIONS of the compass caused by the aggregate influence of the ship's iron upon the magnetic needle, according to the direction of the ship's head.

We have already seen how the 1st, 2nd, 3rd and 4th classes of errors can be eliminated: there remains but to explain the manner of determining the Deviation.

1. Every ship *should be* provided with a standard compass, mounted as before described, and by which all bearings should be taken; as, however, no standard compass has yet been introduced in our vessels, but, on the contrary, the Binnacle Compass is mounted in such a manner as to prevent any bearings being observed with it (especially in the Iron-Clads,) and as the said Binnacle Compass is the one the deviation of which is required to be known, we will suppose, in the following rules, an Azimuth Compass to be used for observing the bearings, and compared with the Binnacle Compass at each observation.

2. When the ship is ready for sea, with her guns, shot and all her iron stores on board and stowed in their proper places, as well as the stanchions and other iron work secured in the positions in which it is intended they shall remain at sea,—then the deviation of the Binnacle Compass from the real magnetic meridian, is to be ascertained by one of the following methods,— and either of which, if the ship be in a basin, can be executed at any time, but if riding in a tideway, at slack water only.

FIRST METHOD.

3. The requisite warps being prepared, the ship is to be gradually swung round, so as to bring her head successively upon each of the 32 points of the compass; and as it approaches each of these points, so gently to check her motion as to prevent any continued swing of the card. When quite steady, and her head exactly on any one point, *by the Binnacle Compass,* observe with the Azimuth Compass (which is supposed to be mounted on the upper deck) the bearing of some distant but well-defined point, and the direction of the ship's head-register, as shown in the Form, Table I., page 45.

4. The ship's head is then to be gently brought (*by the Binnacle Compass* as before) to the next point, and when duly stopped and steadied there, the bearing of the same object and

ship's head by Azimuth Compass again registered; and so on, point after point, till the exact bearing of the one object has been taken with the ship's head on every point of the Compass.

5. The object selected for that purpose should be at such a distance from the ship, that the diameter of the space through which she revolves, shall make no sensible difference in its real bearing—say 6 or 8 miles if riding in a tide way.

6. Having taken the foregoing observations, the next step is to find the *true* magnetic bearing of the object.

This may generally be assumed to be the mean of all the observed bearings—another way is to place the Azimuth Compass on shore, (taking care that there is no iron in the neighbourhood to affect it,) in a line with the object and place where the Azimuth Compass stood during the observations, and then take the bearing—or, if provided with a Harbor Chart, plot the position of the ship and take the bearing of the object from the Chart and *apply the variation* to obtain the correct Magnate Bearing.

In order to determine whether the compass on shore is effected by iron in the neighbourhood or soil, put up a mark at any distance, and take the bearing of it; then, leaving a staff to mark the spot, remove the compass to the mark and observe the reverse bearing—if the bearings are reciprocal, the compass may be supposed to be un-affected at both places—or, observe a set of Azimuths with the Compass on shore and compare the variation found with that given by the Chart.

7. The difference between this real magnetic bearing and the successive bearings of the object by the Binnacle Compass (which bearings are to be *deduced* from the bearings of the Azimuth Compass and heading* of the ship, by both compasses) will show the Deviation of the Binnacle Compass for each point.

Enter these differences as shown in Table I., page 84.

8. The deviation thus found, is to be named *East*, when the North end of the needle is drawn to the Eastward, or right hand, by the attraction of the ship's iron, and *West* when it is drawn to the Westward, or to the left hand, of the magnetic meridian, and is to be applied to a course *in the same manner as the variation.*

EXAMPLE. Ship's head by Binnacle Compass N. E., *deviation* for that course 6° W., therefore the real magnetic deviation of her head will be N. E. ½ N., or N. 39° E.

* Registering the ship's head, by both the Azimuth and Binnacle Compasses, is simply a *comparison* of those Compasses. The bearing of the object by the Azimuth Compass, $\mp$ the difference in the ship's heading by both Compasses, will give the bearing of the object by the Binnacle Compass.

Having Variation and Deviation to apply, if they are of the same name, take their *sum* and apply it; if of different names, take their difference and apply according to the name of the greater.

NOTE. If the Azimuth Compass *is always put up in the same place*, its deviation should also be taken and tabulated; then in taking bearings it will only be necessary to apply the deviation of the Azimuth Compass, to get the true Magnetic Bearing; and reducing the bearings to the Binnacle Compass will be unnecessary, as the results will manifestly be the same.

9. All bearings observed with the Azimuth Compass and reduced to the Binnacle Compass (by noting ship's head by each at the time when said bearings are taken) must be corrected by the deviation which is due to the direction of the ship's head (by the Binnacle Compass) at the moment that they were taken.

10. If it be required to shape a certain *magnetic course* and for that purpose to determine what will be the corresponding *course by the Binnacle Compass*, recollect that this is the *reverse* of the operation given above.

NOTE.—The deviation of the Binnacle Compass having been determined, it must thereafter be considered the "Standard," and must not be moved the *fraction of an inch*. If the compass is supplied with more than one card, remember to note the card used when swinging the ship. It is evident that the deviation of both Binnacle Compasses, or indeed of any number of compasses, can be determined at one swinging by noting the heading of the ship by each compass at every point—this is in fact simply a comparison of the compasses.

When a ship is provided with a "Standard Compass," so placed as to admit of bearings being taken with it, and to use as a steering compass also, it is usual to tabulate the deviations of that compass alone, and to correct all the others by it.

If your vessel is not provided with such a compass—so placed—the simplest plan will be to follow the directions given in the text. Select a mid-ship Binnacle Compass for *your standard*, and avoid bothering yourself with too many compasses.

One Binnacle Compass, *placed on the midship line*, will be more accurate than two, and is all that is required for our iron clads.

SECOND METHOD.

11. Should there be no suitable object visible from the ship and at the requisite distance, the deviations must be ascertained by the process of Reciprocal Bearings. A careful observer must go on shore with a second compass and place its tripod in some open spot (but strictly under the conditions enumerated in Article 6,) and where it may be distinctly seen from the azimuth compass on board. Then, by means of preconcerted signals, the mutual bearings of those two compasses from each other are to be observed at the moment the ship's head (by Binnacle compass) is quietly steady on each of the 32 points suc-

cessively, as directed in the First Method—observing to note the heading of the ship by the azimuth compass at each observation. The mode of registering the observations is shown in Table II., page 85.

12. To ensure the success of this operation the compass on shore should be near enough to be distinctly visible with the naked eye. The observations should be made as strictly simultaneous as possible; and to guard against mistakes the times should be noted by both observers, by compared watches.

13. The compass used on shore should be compared with the azimuth compass and its index error noted.

NOTE.—If you should not be able to procure an Azimuth Compass and tripod for observing the bearings on shore, fit two "sight vanes" on one of your spare compasses, in a line with the "lubber's mark," and use a barrel to set it upon; observing that all of the iron nails should first be drawn from the barrel.

In comparing the compasses, set them up on shore, ten or twelve feet apart, and take the bearing of some distant object; the difference will be the Index Error of the shore compass, which mark *East* if it is to be applied to the right; otherwise, *West*.

14. From the observations thus made, by either of the processes which have been described, a table of the results should be forthwith constructed for general use, and copied by every person on board who keeps a reckoning. The best form for it is given in Table III, where by comparing the 1st with the 3rd column, the courses shown by the Binnacle compass are convertible by inspection into correct magnetic courses. The second column shows the deviation which is to be applied to all the *courses* and *bearings* taken by the Binnacle compass. (See Article 9 and *Note*.)

15. This table shows also the points of *no* deviation, and, if at sea the ship's head be put on one or the other of these points, and an azimuth or amplitude be observed, the variation found will be the *correct magnetic variation*—but with her head on any other point, the variation found must be corrected for the deviation due to that point, to get the correct variation.

16. We readily see from what is said in the preceding article how it is possible to examine the correctness of the "deviation table" at sea, by observing azimuths with the ship's head on different points of the compass and deducing the deviation; for the variation found is equal to the correct magnetic variation (supposed to be given by our chart) plus or minus the deviation.

NOTE.—A "deviation table" may be constructed at sea, in a steamer, by observing azimuths with the ship's head on every point of the compass successively. Then assuming the *mean of the variations found* to be the correct magnetic variation; the *deviation* on each point is equal to the correct magnetic variation, minus the variation found with the ship's head on that point.

17. Calling V the correct magnetic variation (that is the variation of the compass, unaffected by local attraction); V' the variation found with the ship's head on any particular point, and S the deviation for that point, we will always have: $S = V \pm V'$; according as they are of the same, or of different names.

NOTE.—The following will serve as a specimen of the instructions to be given to the officer who is to take the observations on shore. (Second Method.)

For the Officer on shore (*Mem.*)

"When the flag *is* hoisted at the main (or shown behind the observer at the Azimuth Compass on board.) "prepare to observe." Indicate that you are ready by placing your flag in the rear of the observer. The *instant* that the flag is hauled down (or is dipped,) observe, and register the *time and bearing*. If by any accident you fail to get the observation, keep your flag flying, and the flag will be again run up to "prepare to observe"—otherwise, lower your flag after each observation. It is intended to take *three* observations on each heading, but more *may* be taken.

Should you wish to repeat an observation *at any time*, show your flag in the rear of the observer. If you wish to indicate "that you do not understand the signal," or that "you wish to communicate," or that "an accident has happened to your compass," send the flag bearer some distance to the right of your compass.

If the wind does not cause your flag to blow out clear, let a "hand" steady it. When the flag is hoisted at the fore, (or is waived) return on board.

Should you move your position, *mark the observation*.

Take on shore: Note book and pencil, spy glass, spare silk for sight vane, compass, barrel, camp-stool, watch (compared,) flag and staff.

Observations for determining the effect of the ship's iron on the "Binnacle Compass" on board the U. S. S. Merrimack, January 11th, 1859, at Realejo, Nicaragua.

Real Magnetic Bearing of Monotombo, N. 87°, 27' E., distant 20 miles.

TABLE I.—*Form for registering the First Method, by One Direct Bearing*—See Article 7.

(Card A used on Binnacle Compass.)

Ship's Head by Binnacle Compass.	Ship's Head by Azimuth Compass.	Bearing of Monotombo by Binnacle Compass.	Bearing of Monotombo by Azimuth Compass.	Deviation of Binnacle Compass.
North.	N. 2°, E.	N. 89°, 40', E.	N. 91°, 40' E.	2°, 13' W.
N. by E.	N. 13°, 30', E.	90.00	92.15	2, 43 W.
N. N. E.	N. 25°, 30', E.	91 30	94 30	4, 03 W.
N. E. by N.	N. 36°, 45', E.	91.40	94.40	4, 13 W.

And in like manner at all points of the compass.

NOTE.—The Azimuth Compass was mounted on deck, and the "bearings" observed with it and entered in Col. 4. The ship's head was steadied on each point *by the Binnacle Compass*. and the heading of the ship by the Azimuth Compass at the same time, entered in Col. 2.

The Bearings in Col. 3 *are deduced* from Cols. 1, 2 and 4; and the "deviations" from Col. 3, and the real magnetic bearing of Monotombo.

Observations for determining the effect of the ship's iron on the "Binnacle Compass" on board U.S.S. Merrimack, January 11th, 1859, at Realejo, Nicaragua.

Comparison of Azimuth and Shore-compasses made on shore:

Bearing of a distant object by Azimuth Compass, N. 40° E.
do   do   Shore   do   N. 39° E.

Correction to be applied to Shore Compass Bearings, 1° E.

TABLE II.—*Form for registering the Second Process, by Reciprocal Bearings*—See Art. 11.

(Card B used on Binnacle Compass.)

Time.	Ship's Head by Binnacle Compass.	Ship's Head by Azimuth Compass.	Bearing of Shore-compass by Azimuth Compass.	Bearing of Shore-compass by Binnacle Compass.	Bearing of Azimuth Compass from Shore-compass. Observed.	Bearing of Azimuth Compass from Shore-compass. Corrected.	Deviation of the Binnacle Compass.
h. m.							
9.00	North.	N. 2° E.	S. 38° 11' W.	S. 36° 11' W.	N. 33° 01' E.	N. 34° 01' E.	2° 13' W.
9.03	N. by E.	N. 13° 30' E.	S. 36° 22' W.	S. 34° 07' W.	N. 30° 27' E.	N. 31° 27' E.	2° 40' W.
9.06	N. N. E.	N. 25° 30' E.	S. 35° 20' W.	S. 32° 20' W.	N. 27° 30' E.	N. 28° 30' E.	3° 50' W.
9.10	N. E. by N.	N. 36° 45' E.	S. 33° 23' W.	S. 30° 23' W.	N. 25° 03' E.	N. 26° 03' E.	4° 20' W.

And in like manner at all the points of the compass.

NOTE.—The Azimuth Compass was mounted as before. At each observation enter the time, the ship's head by the Azimuth and Binnacle Compass, and the bearing of the shore-compass by the Azimuth Compass. The bearing of shore-compass by the Binnacle Compass is deduced from Cols. 2, 3 and 4. The "Deviation" is deduced from Col. 5, and the *corrected* Bearings in Col. 6.

TABLE III—*Form for tabulating the Results; or the Deviation Table for the U. S. S. Merrimack.*

Ship's Head, or Course by the Binnacle Compass.	Deviation of the Binnacle Compass.	Real Magnetic Course steered.
North.	2°. 10′ W.	N. 2°. 10′ W.
N. by E.	2°. 40′ W.	N. 8°. 55′ E.
N. N. E.	3°. 50′ W.	N. 18°. 40′ E.
N. E. by N.	4°. 20′ W.	N. 29°. 25′ E.
N. E.	5°. 00′ W.	N. 40°. 00′ E.
N. E. by E.	5°. 10′ W.	N. 51°. 05′ E.
E. N. E.	5°. 20′ W.	N. 62°. 10′ E.
E. by N.	5°. 40′ W.	N. 73°. 05′ E.

And so on for all the points.

NOTE.—If the position of the compass is changed; or if any change is made in the disposition of the guns, or any iron on board; or if the ship changes her geographical position considerably, *a new deviation table must be constructed.*

Professor Barlow appears to have first attempted to correct the deviations by a mass of iron placed near the compass. After determining the deviation, he placed a double disk of iron in such a position abaft each compass, as to counteract the influence of the iron of the ship; the position being carefully determined by experiment. It served as a partial corrective for the disturbance by the soft iron of the ship.

In 1839, Prof. Airy proposed, for iron ships especially, in which the deviations were very great, to place in the deck, below it, or above it, or on the binnacle:

1st. A permanent magnet athwart ship, with its centre on a fore and aft line drawn through the joint, directly under the pivot of the compass needle. This is moved along the line, until the compass points correctly with the ship's head N. or S.

2nd. A permanent magnet fore and aft, with its centre on a line athwart ship through the same point. This is moved along the line until the compass is corrected with the ship's head E. or W.

3rd. On a level with the compass and over one of the lines just mentioned, as may be found best on trial, and with one end directly towards the compass, a small box, containing small iron chain, or pieces of soft iron, (provided they are not all laid in the same direction,) so as to correct the deviation with the ship's head on a four point course.

These may be approximately adjusted while swinging the ship for determining the deviations, provided the true magnetic bearing of the object observed on is known. A second trial may complete the adjustment. The boxes containing the magnets and soft iron should then be secured against all danger of disturbance.

Such corrections can only be partially successful. They serve to reduce the deviations, but are not to be relied on implicitly; nor do they render a table of deviations, or occasional tests or correction of it unnecessary. The magnets should be under the control of the Master, so that he can re-adjust them when necessary.

In the sea-ports of England and other countries, there are to be found persons who make it their business to correct compasses for the local attraction; using magnates for the purpose. The Master must not, however, forget that if the vessel changes her geographical position considerably, and *particularly if she crosses the Equator*, the compasses must be again adjusted, and a new table of deviations constructed.

As the compasses in our iron-clad vessels are so placed as to prevent "bearings" being taken with them, it would be convenient if "Bearing-Plates" were provided to ship in a socket on the Turret, or other convenient plea for observing bearings. The following description of a "Bearing Plate," is taken from Captain Johnson's work on "The Deviations of the Compass:"

"The bearing-plate is simply a circular plate of brass (or it may be of zinc or copper) on which the points, and the half and quarter points of the compass, are engraved (but not lettered,) the circumference being graduated, and having the two zeros opposite to each other, and 90° marked at right angles.

"A brass bar capable of a circular movement is attached at the centre of the plate, like that of a circumferenter with a nonius, a perpendicular vane being fixed to each end.

"A double joint underneath the plate, and fitted to an oblong square stem, enables the observer to level the instrument sufficiently near by the eye, for the practical purpose contemplated, the joint affording two vertical motions, one fore and aft and the other athwart-ships.

"Two or three sockets, or oblong troughs, are made very exactly to suit the stem, and so that they may be let into the wood and fixed in any part of the ship, which may be found most convenient for taking bearings. Be it observed, that before fixing the sockets, great care must be taken in adjusting them in the line of the keel, or parallel to it (according to the position selected,) when the vanes of the plates are set to the zeros, and representing that line.

"The stem of the bearing-plate being so constructed that it will only fit one way into the socket, and that while the zeros are accurately in the fore and aft line, no further adjustment in this respect is required at the time of observation. It can, of course, be moved from one socket to another at pleasure, or be taken away altogether, as circumstances may require.

"By means of the above-mentioned contrivance, it will be obvious to the practical navigator that the angle between any objects, lights, land-marks, &c., and the ship's head, may be measured at any time within small limits of error: and hence, by applying that angle to the direction of the ship's head, as indicated at the moment by the standard (or Binnacle) Compass and corrected for deviation, the *correct* magnetic bearing of such objects may be obtained, and which is of the highest importance when navigating intricate channels.

"In very high latitudes, where the dip is great, and the compass becomes useless, the azimuth circle of the standard compass, and likewise the bearing-plate, will be useful appendages for regulating the ship's course by means of the observed angles between the ship's head and the heavenly bodies, and which cannot always be conveniently accomplished by means of the sextant.

FORM OF REPORT TO OFFICE OF ORD. AND N'DY.

A Table of the Deviations of the —— Compass on board the C. S. ——— of —— Guns, ascertained at ———————, by (*here enter the method;*) on the (*here enter the date.*)

Direction of Ship's Head by Compass.	Deviation of Compass.	Comparison with other Compasses.		
		Ship's Head by Compass.	Ship's Head by Compass.	Ship's Head by Compass.
North.				
N. by E.				
N. N. E.				
N. E. by N.				
N. E.				
N. E. by E.				
E. N. E.				
E. by N.				
East.				
&c., &c., &c.				

Mention in the Report the name of the Commander, and by whom the observations were made. Insert the name of the Compass, the deviations of which are reported, and also those compared. State the exact positions of the compasses in the ship; the distance from nearest iron; from funnel; whether forward of the centre of the ship or not; distance from nearest gun; distance between the binnacles; height of cards from the deck; the number and kind of guns and their position, and any other applicable remarks.

There is a method (known among mathematicians as the method of "Least Squares,) by which the *most probable values* of the deviations from observations made on 4, 8, 16 and 32 points can be deduced. It is too long for insertion here; but, if after having made their observations, Masters will enclose the results to the School Ship, the values will be calculated by the author and returned.

It is not always convenient to get the observations on all the points, though it is better to do so—especially if the deviations be great.

If observations are made on 8 points, they should be: N., N. E., E., S. E.; S., S. W., W., and N. W.; if on 4 points, N. E., N. W., S. E. and S. W.

This method will be explained in a future edition of this book.

MASTER'S DUTIES—AT SEA.

NOTE. Th Master should inform the officer of the deck as soon as he takes the *departure*, so that he can commence marking the slate.

The routine at sea is the same as in port, in relation to examining the state of the rigging, winding up Chronometers, serving out wood and water, visiting the holds, keeping the expenditures, writing up the Log, regulating the ship's time, (which is *apparent*, and the deck time-piece is set every day at meridian,) examining lashings of anchors, &c., &c., &c.

The Master should be up and ready to take his morning observations by 7 A. M. The daily observations consist generally of:—

1. Morning observations for time.
2. Meridian observations for latitude.
3. P. M. observations for time.
4.   do.   for variation of the compass.
5. or, sunset observations for variation of the compass.

The "Reckoning" is sent in to the Captain at 8 A. M., meridian, and 8 P. M., unless far away from land, when it is sent in but at meridian.

Constant attention should be paid to the Binnacles and Compasses.

The Master should be able to calculate the position of the ship at any hour, day *or night*, and should therefore be familiar enough with the heavenly bodies to select those required for observation.

The following Forms for keeping your work, will be found convenient at sea. Rule up your book for a number of days in advance, before leaving port, as follows:

Oct.   1863.

A.	Chro. 2971, *or* A.	Sec.	H. D.
		Corr.	
L. sec.	Face.	Corr. Dec.	
	Error.		90.00.00
P. D. __cosec.	Gr. Time.	P. D.	
S.			
½ s. cos.			
A.	Chro. 1858, *or* B.	Eq. Time.	H. D.
Rem. sin.	Face.	Corr.	
2)	Error.	Corr. E. T.	
sin.	Gr. Time.		
App. Time.		Lat. Obs.	
Eq. T.	Chro. 3411, *or* C.	" D. R.	
Mean Time.	Face.	Long. Chro.	
	Error.	" D. R.	
Gr. Time.	Gr. Time.		
Long. in Time.		Var.	
Long.		Current.	
		Lee Way.	

After taking your morning observations, sum up and take the mean; correct the altitude, and find the Greenwich time and enter both in your Form. Take out the Dec. and Equation of Time, correct both, find the Polar Distance and enter them—take out and enter the Cosecant of the Polar Distance. Enter the time of each Chronometer with its error and you have the Greenwich Time by each: the mean of which enter in column 1, to use in finding the Longitude. Enter the Variation and Lee-Way in column 3.

All this should be done soon after taking the observations: that is, before 11 o'clock. After the log slate has been marked at 6 bells, work up the "Dead Reckoning," (estimating the course and distance for the hour from 11 to meridian,) and enter the Latitude and Longitude D. R. in column 3 of your book. Correct the Declination for the Longitude, and you are ready for the meridian observation.

Working up the day's work, &c., can be done on a slate—it is not necessary to keep a copy, as it can always be worked over from the Log-Book.

As soon as you have obtained the Latitude by Mer. Alt. work it back to the time of morning observations, enter it in column 1, and calculate the apparent time.

Blank Forms should be prepared for your Reports to the Captain beforehand.

By adopting the above system, your reckoning will be in the cabin in ten minutes after meridian, and you will always be able to refer back to your work. You can distinguish your two books as "Record" and "Note." The deck time-piece must be set at 12 o'clock. In estimating the distance the ship will probably run between the hours of 11 and 12, do not forget that if running to the Eastward you will make a "short" hour; if to the Westward a "long" one.

Masters should, at sea, occasionally find the ship's position by Lunars, Double Altitudes, Sumner's Method, Altitude near noon, &c., and compare it with that found by A. M. and meridian observations, in order to be able to estimate the *probable error* in case the chronometers should run down, or the sun be obscured at meridian.

If, however, you should allow your chronometers to run down, I would advise *starting them by the Longitude D. R.* in preference to "Lunars;" unless in a strong current, the direction of which you do not know.

The Master should be able to distinguish all the Lunar Stars, though the distance between the *sun* and moon will give a better result than a night observation, if you have the choice.

Don't fail to use the moon in finding the Latitude and Longitude, especially if you can get the observation just after, or before sunrise or sunset.

Accustom yourself to night observations and tabulate them, for reference as to their accuracy.

In some Latitudes you may be forced to rely upon night observations altogether, therefore be prepared by constantly practicing beforehand.

In case of making known land, an opportunity is afforded of "testing" the chronometers which should be taken advantage of. Navigators very frequently "sight" land for this purpose: vessels from Boston to Madeira, for instance, sight the Peak of

Pico (Azores;) and outward-bound Indiamen from England the Peak of Teneriffe, or Island of St. Vincent, (Cape de Verdes.)

A set of observations immediately after leaving port, will satisfy the Master whether his chronometers are correct.

The Log lines should be frequently measured and corrected—especially if new—and upon nearing the land, the deep-sea lead and line and hand-leads and lines should be gotten ready.

While at sea, the Master should study the harbor chart of the port to which he is bound, and should inform himself of the prevailing winds; currents; depth of water; rise and fall of tides, &c., &c., and, just before entering, should calculate the time of high water—bearing in mind that he will probably have to *pilot the ship in himself.*

He should be able to answer all questions relating to the port and its anchorages; such as facilities for getting wood and water; depth of water at anchorage; from which direction are gales to be expected; (as, if the vessel is to be *moored*, the executive officer will require to be informed on the point, so as to lie with an "open hawse,") names of head-lands, &c., &c., &c.

Upon making the land, the Master should attend personally to getting the anchors off the bows and ranging the chains: reporting to the officer of the deck and executive officer when they are ready.

He should establish his position frequently by "cross bearings," as the vessel closes in with her port.

After anchoring, "plot," the position of your anchorage on the harbor chart, tend to duties as prescribed, &c., &c., &c.

In the foregoing article, it is not to be supposed that *all* the Master's duties have been alluded to. Many others will, doubtless, suggest themselves.

The young officer, however, who thoroughly understands what has been written, and diligently attends to the "hints" given, will be in a fair way of becoming a good Master and navigator.

INDEX.

PART I.

Rigging. Questions on,	5

PART II.

HARBOR ROUTINE:

	PAGE
Daily Routine in Port,	8
Upon "Taking the Deck" in Port,	11
Stowing Hammocks,	12
Piping Down Hammocks,	12
Getting up Hammock Girt-Lines and Clothes-Lines, and Stopping on Hammocks, or Clothes,	13
To Spread the Awnings, &c.,	15
Hoisting and Lowering Boats,	16
Morning and Evening Quarters,	17
Squaring Yards.	18
To Scrape the Light Spars, &c.,	20
Airing Bedding,	21
To get the Lower Booms out,	21
Making and Answering Signals,	22
To Loose Sails,	24
To Furl Sails,	25
To Cross Top-Gallant and Royal Yards,	27
To send down the Top-Gallant and Royal Yards,	28
To Cross Top-Gallant and Royal Yards, and Loose Sail,	28
To send up, and down, the Top-Gallant Masts,	29
To send up Top-Gallant Masts, and Cross Top-Gallant Yards,	31
To send down Top-Gallant Masts, and Yards,	31
To send up Top Gallant Masts, and Loose Sails,	32
To send up Top-Gallant Masts and Yards, and Loose Sails,	33
To Mend Sails,	33
Hoisting in and out Boats,	33
Bending and Unbending Sails,	35
Boat Service,	36
Military Honors and Ceremonies,	37
Hoisting in Provisions, Water, &c.,	39
Serving out Provisions, Clothing, Small Stores, &c. Instructions on,	41

PART III.

EVOLUTIONS:

Tacking,	43
Wearing,	45
Wind Hauling Aft,	50
Wind Hauls Forward,	52

PART IV.

MASTER'S DUTIES:

Hints for Young Masters,	62
Master,	63
Master's Duties—In Port,	68
Memorandum,	73
To find the Deviation of the Compass,	79
First Method,	80
Second Method,	82
Table I,	84
Table II,	85
Table III,	86
Form of Report to Office of Ordnance and Hydrography,	88
Master's Duties—At Sea,	89

www.ingramcontent.com/pod-product-compliance
Lightning Source LLC
Chambersburg PA
CBHW031604110426
42742CB00037B/1106